Soteriology

The Total Walk Of Salvation

by

Scott C. Lovett

Fervent Fire Productions

Tulsa, Oklahoma

This book was printed at a driven pace
due to high demand.
We acknowledge errors in punctuation,
grammar, and clarity of writing.
All of these issues will be rectified.

- Fervent Fire Productions

Unless otherwise indicated, all Old and New Testament Scripture quotations are taken from the *King James Version, 1769 edition* of the Bible.

Soteriology

ISBN#9781495152658

Fervent Fire Evangelistic Ministries

315 S. Sheridan Road

Tulsa, OK 74112

Published by Fervent Fire Productions

315 S. Sheridan Road

Tulsa, OK 74112

Dedication

To Jesus Christ, my God, my King, the only God who lived perfectly defeating the sin nature of man through His sacrifice and atoning work on the cross. To all of the men of God who preached true salvation to men in order to restore man back to God through their work of obedience to the Holy Spirit. To all people who have previously dedicated their lives to Jesus Christ in order to bear His image. To those who are about to start the most magnificent relationship they have ever encountered.

Scott C. Lovett

Contents

Introduction

The definition of what it is to be a "Christian" in American society has become so obscure that the true nature and identity of Jesus Christ within the life of the masses of the so called converted is hard to perceive. The Greek word "christianos" means, "A follower of Christ and His teachings, one carrying the anointing, and one who submits to Christ's ownership." This single word defines and brings clarity to those who say they are Christian. The responsibility of being a Christian is not one that is without education, discipline and purpose. In fact, the core idea of being a Christian is the root of ownership. The idea of God owning us is not one that is popular in the present day culture. Everyone wants to believe they are good at heart, but when it comes to human nature this is not the case. True salvation is the work that builds the ownership of Christ into the heart of mankind to do God's will on the earth. The anointing is applied and power is released as the believer submits to the will of God, enthusiastically obeying the Word and yielding to the Holy Spirit, thereby breaking the rebellious nature and sinful will.

Christianity is not a free pass to fulfill the desires of the flesh, but it remains the act of following Jesus to lay your life down and commit to a far greater life that leads to the fulfillment of knowing you did the Father's will.

The term "Christian" is not only obscure within the lives of men, but it has also become vague and watered down behind the American pulpit. The offer of salvation is one that is simplified to the point that the one making the decision is unaware of any future obligation to God. So much emphasis is placed on the "sinner's prayer" that this simple act is not one of introduction to God, but rather the whole experience of God himself. Denominations, Associations, and local church bodies hold up conversion cards and membership rolls to prove that they have produced something for God. Yet the individual desiring conversion fails to understand the lifelong commitment of relationship with God that it takes to be a Christian. Instant Christianity takes over and the preacher declares salvation over the new convert like a pope giving an indulgence. The new convert receives their stamp of approval, but fails to understand that being a Christian is a lifelong commitment of intimacy with God. True conversion and new birth is the state of new desire and heart felt love for God Himself, not just the act of repeating a prayer. The inward work of redemption from sin causes the old to pass away and a new creature is drawn by the Holy Spirit for the new and great purpose of fulfilling God's will by becoming God's servant on the earth.

While the introduction to God and the moment of conversion is an immediate act of change, the work of salvation is one that needs to be understood and taught. The word Soteriology comes from the two Greek words "soteria" and "logos". In

English, the word "soteria" is salvation it means deliverance from the molestation of the enemy, it is a state of welfare, safety, prosperity, victory, and health. The root of this word is "soter" which is Savior, the one who delivers, saves, and preserves. The Greek word "logos" is the Word which is spoken, written and studied. When these two words come together, they place us on the remarkable road of the study of salvation. It is a study that leads us to understand the work of salvation in its entirety. It is not just the moment of introduction that we must understand, or merely the inward work of desire change, but it is the growth that we become aware of that causes us to press forward to the mark of being like Jesus Christ.

To truly understand salvation we cannot pick and choose the portions of Scripture we want to obey to get it. The safest way is to spend your entire life longing to experience everything inside the pages of the Bible. Denominationalism has taught us to focus on a certain work or experience to get to God. For instance the Methodists have certain methods, the Baptists focus on baptism, the Lutherans on the experience of Martin Luther, the Presbyterians on the idea of plurality of church Government, Episcopalians on the idea of the single overseer directly from Apostolic succession, Faith churches on the single idea of the work of Faith, and so on. No one work is going to save you, but a sincere desire to obey all of Jesus Word is the most sincere way to fulfill God's plan. Man has always desired a quick fix and the easy way out when it comes time to study.

The truth is that denominationalism is nothing more than the spiritual version of Cliff notes. The sin nature wants us to not read and experience the full text of the Word of God in our lives, so we satisfy the spiritual longing by letting the denomination give us a simplified version of the Bible that gets us to heaven the fastest way possible. The truth is when it comes to salvation most of us just want to pass the test. This has never been the intent of God, God wants an actual relationship and has a longing for a people to fulfill His will on the earth. God placed man here to take dominion and rule over God's creation to stop the work of the enemy. Adam allowed mankind to be hijacked by disobeying God and obeying the voice of the devil which made him subservient to the sin nature of the flesh and caused him to separate from God.

Chapter 1

Faith Relationship

Salvation is more than just a moment of simple repenting of sin or speaking the sinner's prayer. The act of salvation is a decision of relationship that restores man back to God. From the beginning, God chose to be in a relationship with us. This relationship was an intimate and loving fellowship, teaching man to nurture and care for His creation through responsibility. Following God's order shows love for God and love for others. God made man in His image as spirit (Genesis 1:26-27), allowing man to have a direct line to the realm of the supernatural. Man could literally walk with God and God with man. By spending time with God, man was destined to learn God's ways. God made man a natural being as well, giving humankind a body formed from the earth (Genesis 2:7) with the ability to take natural dominion. God made man a living soul (Genesis 2:7), the soul being a place where man could think, remember, emote and feel. The soul enabled man to give his will over to the one's he loved in both the natural and supernatural realm. Man, woman, and creation were made by God and pronounced to be good, very good. As long as man fellowshipped and communed with God the state of things "being good," remained, and the earth was literally the Garden of Eden, defined as a place of delight.

Knowing no evil, humankind walked in the cool of the day and knew no lack. As a threefold being, man was not only called to take dominion over the natural earth, but through the simple act of obeying one request from God (Genesis 2:17), man would take spiritual dominion over Lucifer and the fallen angels who had been cast out of heaven (Isaiah 14:12-15, Ezekiel 28:16-18, Jude 1:6, Revelation 12:4, Job 38:7), falling into the earth. Even though Lucifer had been created for good, he desired to be God Himself and sought to overthrow God, instead of yielding to God's purpose and submitting to God's will. Through one rebellious choice, heaven was disrupted and creation lay in the balance. But God had a plan and that plan was to create a being natural and spiritual. Giving the first Adam dominion over the earth, and the keys to its care. The relationship between God and man was one of intimacy, trust, fellowship and friendship where God loved man and man loved God; a place where only good reigned, the demonic was barren, and the earth remained pure under the Holy Spirit's control in a state of joy and peace.

The supernatural side of man not only allowed him to walk with God, but it also opened him up to a simple but crucial test. God gave mankind only one rule to follow; the rule not to eat of the tree of the knowledge of good and evil. As long as man knew only God and His goodness, man would never have to suffer the inward soul struggle of knowing right and wrong. Instead, the flesh would stay in submission to the spirit of man and would stay in a place of the perfect balance of prosperity and health. Satan, being very subtle and crafty, knew that the

14

spirit of man was the key for man to lose his dominion. As a spirit being, he knew if he could twist God's Words, he could fill man with his influence and open him up to knowing good and evil, thereby causing the fall into sin and mankind to be compromised. Adam was the most intimate with God of the two humans, but he was failing to effectively communicate God's will and plan to his spouse, Eve. This failure would open mankind to a fatal error that would not only introduce sin, but continue to work its destruction into generations to come. The error of ineffectively communicating God's Word continues to allow people to be destroyed and satan to generate his lies. By the simple act of satan twisting God's Word, Eve and Adam placed faith in his lie and the act of sin is manifest. This opens the soul up to good and evil causing an internal struggle within man. This struggle brings man into a state of confusion, opening him up to pride and the longing to be God himself under the new found demonic influence. The result is man trying to determine his own truth, fulfill his own selfish desires by yielding to his flesh, thereby bringing destruction to his relationship with God, others, and a breakdown in the earth. The new sin nature that is introduced causes man to feel insecure, naked and vulnerable. It opens man up to the demonic feelings of fear, shame, and doubt concerning God's love and acceptance for him. Man hides and God calls out to him in an effort to restore the relationship, fellowship, and intimacy He has lost. While man hears God call out to him, the sin nature lies and says God no longer loves. Everything feels like chaos after putting faith in satan's words. For relationship with God to be restored, man must believe God's Word over his new sin nature, and trust God's voice by following Him by faith. The door that opened the loss of relationship with God is the door that mankind must return to, to get back to God. Mankind's failure was in listening and placing faith in the wrong voice. Man must overcome the feelings of fear, shame, and doubt and return to God by believing His Words and walking towards Him in faith.

To return to God, man must be retaught the ways of the Spirit and believe God over the nature within himself due to a fallen state. Many people think that faith is simply a term to be used in the church setting, but in reality every person ever born on the face of the earth has pursued their life in some form of faith operation. The operation of faith is simply believing in something. Man is always using his faith to believe something. The act of belief is all around us. It is what causes humans to follow a certain direction or pursue a course of action. Romans 12:3 shows all men have faith when it says, "according as God has dealt to every man the measure of faith." While all men have faith, not all men believe in the Gospel. You can guarantee that all men believe in something. The atheist spends his time believing there is no God. People who make money God, and lust after it, use their faith to believe business success is right around the corner. Those who are overcome with fear tend to release their faith and believe their fears are true. If they believe they are going to be robbed, they will release their finances to install a home security system, fifteen deadbolts, and hire two armed guards. The truth is, humans finance and pursue what they have faith in.

In America, we currently find ourselves in a state of humanistic godlessness simply because people believe the voices inside themselves and the voices of other humans instead of the Word of God. The danger in following men who fail to follow God is that those men are being led by some voice. If the voice is not God then what voice is doing the leading? Be sure it will only lead to the sin nature, which is a way of suffering and pain, even if the road is laid with so called good intentions. To be restored back to God, we must believe the Word and be drawn by the Holy Spirit. Let's take a look at some texts from the Scripture.

John 1:12-13
But as many as received Him, to them gave He power to become the sons of God, even to them that believe on his name: Which were born, not of blood, nor of the will of the flesh, nor of the will of man, but of God.

John 20:27
Then saith he to Thomas, Reach hither thy finger, and behold my hands; and reach hither thy hand, and thrust it into my side: and be not faithless, but believing.

Romans 10:10
For with the heart man believeth unto righteousness; and with the mouth confession is made unto salvation.

Acts 16:31-32

And they said, Believe on the Lord Jesus Christ, and thou shalt be saved, and thy house. And they spake unto him the word of the Lord, and to all that were in his house.

The two main words used in John 1:12 describe the release of man's faith. They are summed up in receive and believe. The Greek word for receive is "lamberno." It means to take and make your own, to procure for yourself, and to strive after. The act of faith is a very personal experience. It starts with the individual desire to make the Gospel and the relationship with God yours. It is a desire of the heart that causes a person to want the goodness of God. As this desire increases, it causes you to believe. The word believe in the Greek is "pisteno." It means to place confidence in, to think to be true, to be convicted of the truth. Of course, we must recognize that the truth being referenced here is the Word of God. It is the message of the Gospel that births this moment and causes people to be restored back to God through this act of faith. While man releases faith to return to God, God is the one in charge of the new birth. The internal work of being born again is not in man's blood, his will, or the nature of his flesh. Spiritual rebirth comes only from God. Instead of believing the voices of the sin nature that make God into a mean spirit to be feared, hearing the Gospel causes man to see God as he truly is; loving, caring, nurturing, and relational: a God who desires to bring us back to a state of restored relationship with Him. The other voices, the demonic spirits, are at work to keep God and man apart. By keeping man from God, the demonic spirits have dominion over men thereby continuing demonic chaos and increasing the curse in the earth itself. Restoration to God is the only way for mankind to come back to a place of ruling out of a heart of love.

True Christianity is not found by simply joining a denomination. It is not found by being born into a specific family or certain race. It is not found in the halls of Government or in religious ceremony. It is not found by simply saying a prayer because someone asks you to. It is found inside the heart of every person who desires to have a relationship with God. This relationship starts with a belief in God and His goodness. It all starts with internal heart felt faith. Not the heart felt faith of a group, but rather the heart felt faith of the individual. While many people want to believe Christianity starts in the halls of religion, the faith chapter in Hebrews gives us a far different picture of those seeking God by relationship.

Hebrews 11:6-8

But without faith it is impossible to please him: for he that cometh to God must believe that he is, and that he is a rewarder of them that diligently seek him. By faith Noah, being warned of God of things not seen as yet, moved with fear, prepared an ark to the saving of his house; by the which he condemned the world, and became heir of the righteousness which is by faith. By faith Abraham, when he was called to go out into a place which he should after receive for an inheritance, obeyed; and he went out, not knowing whither he went.

Salvation is not just a one-time act of profession. It is a state of constant desire to follow after God, seeking His way in all things, following God to the state of His goodness. Since salvation is truly to desire relationship with God, we must be aware that the works of religion without the heart of relationship are truly all in vain. It is not that Christians can't do good works, or that the Holy Spirit does not produce good in men's lives. It is that, without the relationship with God, everything that is to be enjoyed in this life is useless and meaningless. It cannot truly be enjoyed because humankind lives in a state of fear about failure or listens to the multiple demonic voices that lead in circles. We must return to the God, who made it all, to truly understand our purpose and the meaning of this life. As I write this book, I believe millions of people go through the motions of Christianity, Sunday after Sunday, without having an intimate relationship with God. Instead of walking and talking with God, they practice the works of a Christian without knowing the God of Christianity. These works are in vain because they are not mixed with true faith and God is not the one doing the directing. It does not mean the principles of the Word are false, but without knowing God, they don't have the same intimate experience that leads them to become like Christ.

Galatians 2:16

Knowing that a man is not justified by the works of the law, but by the faith of Jesus Christ, even we have believed in Jesus Christ, that we might be justified by the faith of Christ, and not by the works of the law: for by the works of the law shall no flesh be justified.

Hebrews 4:2
For unto us was the gospel preached, as well as unto them: but the word preached did not profit them, not being mixed with faith in them that heard it.

As we move towards understanding all the aspects of salvation, we must first acknowledge the necessity of a true desire to have a restored relationship with God. It is not just about the blessings that go with Christianity, it is about the inward heart that burns to know Him, love Him, and see His will done in the earth. This relationship starts with faith and ends in faith. It is a never ending walk that reveals God in every area of our lives, teaching us who He really is and how much He loves and cares for us. I conclude this chapter with Ephesians 3:17: "That Christ may dwell in your hearts by faith."

Chapter 2

Special People

The idea of obtaining salvation by outward tradition or work is one that keeps people all over the world from experiencing the life transforming power of God that starts in the heart. Practicing religion without relationship with God is like being in a marriage where you do all the natural things necessary to look like you have a great marriage, but lack the inward love to experience every moment from the heart. The sad fact is that this affects the children in the marriage and causes them to replicate the practice. Without filling the inward heart with God's love, the sin nature brings pain because of the lack of love for God. Like parents in a bad marriage, religion teaches congregational children all over the world that this how marriage works. Millions sit in churches each week going through the motions, practicing works based religion. These practices actually hinder response to God and keep God from owning the individual from the heart. Many people go to church and keep the denominational traditions without feeling the intimate relationship with Jesus in the heart. Why does God want man's heart? The heart is the center of our being and is the central location that causes emotion to be released concerning the things you desire and love. If the Truth be known, sin does not generate from the outside of man. It is generated from what is loved, desired, or experienced within the heart.

Mark 7:20-23
And he said, That which cometh out of the man, that defileth the man. For from within, out of the heart of men, proceed evil thoughts, adulteries, fornications, murders, thefts, covetousness, wickedness, deceit, lasciviousness, an evil eye, blasphemy, pride, foolishness: All these evil things come from within, and defile the man.

Proverbs 4:20-23
My son, attend to my words; incline thine ear unto my sayings. Let them not depart from thine eyes; keep them in the midst of thine heart. For they are life unto those that find them, and health to all their flesh. Keep thy heart with all diligence; for out of it are the issues of life.

Psalms 119:11
Thy word have I hid in mine heart, that I might not sin against thee.

Without true love and intimacy for God from the heart, you will continually produce the outward nature of sin. This is why faith in God and his Word is so important. When you love God and his Word inwardly, you are nurturing a relationship that leads you to become more like Jesus Christ, thereby taking on His sin defeating nature. When you merely practice denominational tradition, you fail to become like Christ because you are too busy trying to become what the men of the organization say you should be outwardly. This leads to many of the controversies that may be seen in our day. People have used denomination, organization, party and race to cause men to work to be accepted into the group. Whatever group they belong to appeals to their human need to feel special and wanted. People will literally fight for whatever group they feel they belong to. All of the various groups appeal to the basic human need of being connected. To be accepted, the individual is immediately pressed to conform to the goal or the central purpose of the group. The goal or focus of the group is then is required of the individual. The central beliefs must be kept, even if they go against God's Word. If anyone differs in any way from the set agenda, they are out of the group. This is the mistake the nation of Israel made concerning their relationship with God. The people claimed to be God's chosen race, but failed to love and know the God they were serving from the heart. They went after other gods and still continued to say they were the special people, thinking that the outward traditions were enough to keep God on their side. They were told that, to be special and accepted, they simply did these things on the outside. What they failed to realize is that God looks at the heart.

Deuteronomy 7:6
For thou art an holy people unto the LORD thy God: the LORD thy God hath chosen thee to be a special people unto himself, above all people that are upon the face of the earth.

Exodus 19:5-6

Now therefore, if ye will obey my voice indeed, and keep my covenant, then ye shall be a peculiar treasure unto me above all people: for all the earth is mine: And ye shall be unto me a kingdom of priests, and an holy nation. These are the words which thou shalt speak unto the children of Israel.

When we look at the text in Deuteronomy, it appears at first glance that God is playing partiality or even racism. God did not choose the nation of Israel based on race, political agenda, or even on religious practice. They were chosen based on Abraham's commitment to God through faith. God was honoring relationship with Abraham, who, by the way, originated from another nationality. It wasn't about nationality, denomination, or political system. It was about a relationship with God through faith. In the Exodus text, we see that there were conditions to remain connected with God. The people were told to obey God's voice and keep his covenant. Without covenant relationship with God, it becomes really hard to hear His voice. The covenant relationship God was referring to is the covenant given to Abraham. This covenant is given in Genesis 17:10-11. It says, "This is my covenant, which ye shall keep, between me and you and thy seed after thee; every man child among you shall be circumcised. And ye shall circumcise the flesh of your foreskin; and it shall be a token of the covenant betwixt me and you." Without a heartfelt relationship with God, the generations that followed Abraham thought all they had to do was be physically circumcised to be the chosen, special people. The word in Hebrew for covenant is, "beriyth," which is formed from two primary Hebrew words. One is "barah," which means to cut into; to eat or choose. The other, "bara" means to be created, formed or shaped by cutting. For true covenant to take place, Abraham had to place faith in God's Words. He had to literally consume them. This consumption resulted in a new creation, a new shape to be formed, and it came by cutting. When understood in context with other Scripture, we find that the meaning of the Hebrew word "beriyth" can be summed up as, "choosing to eat God's Word forms a new creation, cutting off the flesh and bringing an alliance of friendship and marriage to God." This idea is further identified to us in the following texts:

Romans 2:28-29
For he is not a Jew, which is one outwardly; neither is that circumcision, which is outward in the flesh: But he is a Jew, which is one inwardly; and circumcision is of the heart, in the spirit, not in the letter; whose praise is not of men, but of God.

Romans 9:6-8
For they are not all Israel, which are of Israel: Neither, because they are the seed of Abraham, are they all children: but, In Isaac shall thy seed be called. That is, they which are the children of the flesh, these are not the children of God: but the children of the promise are counted for the seed.

Deuteronomy 30:6

And the LORD thy God will circumcise thine heart, and the heart of thy seed, to love the LORD thy God with all thine heart, and with all thy soul, that thou mayest live.

Jeremiah 4:4

Circumcise yourselves to the LORD, and take away the foreskins of your heart, ye men of Judah and inhabitants of Jerusalem: lest my fury come forth like fire, and burn that none can quench, because of the evil of your doings.

Romans 4:11

And he received the sign of circumcision, a seal of the righteousness of the faith which he had yet being uncircumcised: that he might be the father of all them that believe, though they be not circumcised; that righteousness might be imputed unto them also.

At the root of religion and denomination is the idea that a particular group is somehow more special or true than those who are with another organization. The idea of true Christianity is to love God so much that you allow His Word to cut the sin nature away from your heart to restore right relationship with God. The mindset that God prefers a certain group of people over others is not a principle generated from God. God is looking for all people to have a relationship with Him. As humans, we love to be identified with the groups with which we are comfortable. But in reality, the Word of God requires us to stop promoting a single group. Instead of grouping people together by race, political affiliation or denomination, we must understand that God unifies His body by each individual desiring a relationship with Him and with others in their local sphere. Out of a relationship with Jesus Christ comes right relationship with others. The problem is that, if we select what *we* want to obey or allow out of the Bible text, we are ultimately building our kingdom and not God's. Over the years I have heard several people tell me that a certain group or race was the true Israel. What they fail to recognize is, they are propagating a replacement theology that makes them Israel over other nationalities, denominations, or people. I want to stop and recognize that there are true descendants from Abraham and that there is a natural Jewish nation. God is honoring His natural promise to Abraham, but that does not mean the natural Jew honors their internal relationship with God. Salvation does not come through the flesh, through race, agenda or through denominational affiliation. It comes from faith in the heart that results in a new creation.

Galatians 6:15 says, "For in Christ Jesus neither circumcision availeth any thing, nor uncircumcision, but a new creature." Instead of trying to make our group special, we must understand that Salvation is to all. Let's take a look at the following texts.

John 1:7
The same came for a witness, to bear witness of the Light, that all men through him might believe.

John 12:32

And I, if I be lifted up from the earth, will draw all men unto me.

Acts 17:30-31

And the times of this ignorance God winked at; but now commandeth all men every where to repent: because he hath appointed a day, in the which he will judge the world in righteousness by that man whom he hath ordained; whereof he hath given assurance unto all men, in that he hath raised him from the dead.

Romans 5:18

Therefore as by the offence of one judgment came upon all men to condemnation; even so by the righteousness of one the free gift came upon all men unto justification of life.

1 Timothy 2:3-4

For this is good and acceptable in the sight of God our Saviour; Who will have all men to be saved, and to come unto the knowledge of the truth.

1 Timothy 4:10

For therefore we both labour and suffer reproach, because we trust in the living God, who is the Saviour of all men, specially of those that believe.

Titus 2:11-14

For the grace of God that bringeth salvation hath appeared to all men, Teaching us that, denying ungodliness and worldly lusts, we should live soberly, righteously, and godly, in this present world; Looking for that blessed hope, and the glorious appearing of the great God and our Saviour Jesus Christ; Who gave himself for us, that he might redeem us from all iniquity, and purify unto himself a peculiar people, zealous of good works.

2 Peter 3:9

The Lord is not slack concerning his promise, as some men count slackness; but is longsuffering to us-ward, not willing that any should perish, but that all should come to repentance.

After looking at the texts above, we see that Jesus Christ died for all. He did not come to save a special people or a certain group. The idea that God chooses some and rejects others has been taught and propagated in some denominational circles. Some call it the doctrine of predestination. The problem with this doctrine is that it fails to explain why God would let His "choosing power" allow Adam and Eve to be plucked out of His hand to sin in the first place. According to Scripture, man sins when "he is drawn away by his own lust." This is known as the sin nature. Yet, Adam and Eve, who were completely controlled by the Spirit of God, still had the ability to lust before falling into the sin nature. The problem is not in the fact that Adam and Eve sinned, but rather in the doctrine of "pre-*destined*-nation." If we use these words in this way, we can clearly see that it is replacement theology in disguise. Earlier in Deuteronomy 7:6, we recall that "God hath chosen thee to be a special people unto himself." The problem is not in the idea of being used by God, but rather in the idea of being chosen. The word chosen in the Hebrew is "bacher." It means to choose, to test, to try, to examine. In the New Testament, the word is "eklegomai," which means to choose, call out to, to be picked out. The question is, who has the power of choice? In the Hebrew word, we see the idea of proving, trying, and examining. The New Testament word reveals a calling out. The truth is that God is calling out, but each one of us have to choose the relationship as well. Jesus called out to each of His disciples and said, "Come follow me." Each one had to make a decision to believe His words and follow His ways. There are some disciples who left when His Words were too much for them to handle (John 6:60-68). Even Judas was selected, but his nature was of another spirit. The word "chosen," at first glance, seems to indicate that God is playing partiality. But in reality, it can mean, "You choose to hear my voice, believe and obey, and I choose to walk with you." Another word that comes from the same root is the word, "election." Let's take a look at the following text.

2 Peter 1:10-11
Wherefore the rather, brethren, give diligence to make your calling and election sure: for if ye do these things, ye shall never fall: For so an entrance shall be ministered unto you abundantly into the everlasting kingdom of our Lord and Saviour Jesus Christ.

This text clearly places the responsibility of those following God back on their ability to hear and obey God in faith. Relationship requires something of us. It is not just one sided, but like a marriage or a friendship that requires both parties to come into agreement. The Christian is to agree with God's Word. By doing so we develop a relationship with Jesus Christ who is the Word with which we agree. While I do not believe in the doctrine of God picking some people and leaving others out, I do believe that all men were predestined. We were predestined to bear the image and nature of God. We were called to be like Him and defeat the demonic forces of hell. True predestination is not about God picking people, but it is about people from every nation, tongue, tribe, and kindred restoring their relationship to God so they can live in His goodness. The opportunity has been given; the Way has been set. All we have to do is walk in it.

Romans 8:29-30
For whom he did foreknow, he also did predestinate to be conformed to the image of his Son, that he might be the firstborn among many brethren. Moreover whom he did predestinate, them he also called: and whom he called, them he also justified: and whom he justified, them he also glorified.

1 John 3:1-3

Behold, what manner of love the Father hath bestowed upon us, that we should be called the sons of God: therefore the world knoweth us not, because it knew him not. Beloved, now are we the sons of God, and it doth not yet appear what we shall be: but we know that, when he shall appear, we shall be like him; for we shall see him as he is. And every man that hath this hope in him purifieth himself, even as he is pure.

Colossian 3:10-11

And have put on the new man, which is renewed in knowledge after the image of him that created him: Where there is neither Greek nor Jew, circumcision nor uncircumcision, Barbarian, Scythian, bond nor free: but Christ is all, and in all.

You were made to bear God's image and to take on His nature by learning about and walking in God through the Word and the Spirit. You are predestined to defeat every one of your enemies and glorify your God. You are one of God's Special people if you desire a relationship with God, seek the Father's will and develop a heartfelt love for others.

Chapter 3

The Five Solas

While there are many individual views on the doctrine of salvation, we must endeavor to receive the full Truth from the Word of God. In this hour, people are distorting the truth to the point that all men have been labeled Christian even though many of them have no real relationship with, or feeling towards God. The truth is, Jesus is salvation, and to know salvation is to know the Saviour. In our day, we have moved away from knowing Him personally to knowing Him through what an organization says about salvation. Within the world of the church, there are two main doctrines that exist about salvation. One is the doctrine of Calvinism (spoken through the lips and the teaching of John Calvin) and other is the doctrine of Arminianism (spoken through the lips of Jacob Arminius). Neither of these men's names are in the Bible, yet we have named doctrines after them. As Christians, we should be encouraged to know God through His Word, not just through the individual thoughts or opinions of men.

The total work of salvation is not just given to you through a simple prayer. It is a lifelong pursuit of God. There are many people who attended church one time in their life and said the sinner's prayer and never reflected the fruit of a life committed to God. Yet we find ministers who will boldly declare them saved. There are also people who faithfully attend church and have the outward signs of Christianity down, who will stand before the Lord and not enter in to heaven due to knowing religion rather than God. As a minister of the Gospel, my job is to preach the Word of God, not to declare people saved. Only Jesus Christ has the power to save and know them that are His. Each of us must know we are committed to God from within ourselves. Only God can know our hearts, and true believers ask God to search their hearts and deal with them because they value their relationship. We are not called to know God through others, we are called to know God ourselves. Salvation is not something that is declared or placed on you by a man. It is not something attained through joining a denomination or a particular church. No pastor has the right or the ability to pronounce someone saved. Salvation is not bought, it is not rewarded by a single act or a tradition.

The idea of a church or minister pronouncing someone saved is not something that is new. From the time of 312AD, when Emperor Constantine became the head of Rome until now, this practice has been used to allow various people entrance into the church for various reasons. Many were given indulgences based on monetary gifts, while others had connections and were granted special favor. Still others came in as the Romans opened up their version of christianity to the masses. Rome had always conquered countries by allowing the local culture to exist within the context and framework of the local government. The word "culture" is not based in race alone, but rather the acceptance of a people group's social and ethnic beliefs. Instead of renouncing paganism, which is the worship of false gods, idols, people, objects and more, they "purified" it and appropriated it for God's use. It is impossible to purify pagan practices, since they are inspired by the demonic and cause the individuals who practice them to take their eyes off of God and look to another source for the answer to a problem. The Bible exclusively restricts our worship to God and God alone. God strictly forbids things in creation to be worshipped or human beings to be glorified. We don't worship creation, we worship the Creator Himself. We also do not worship men because all men have sin and are, by nature, fallible themselves. This is why it is important to recognize that Jesus is God and sinless. God Himself took a body, walked perfectly in the flesh, fulfilling all Scripture in the flesh, offering Himself as the spotless sacrifice that graced humanity by taking our sin. No other founder of a man made religion claimed to be sinless or God in the flesh. Only Jesus took on the sinful nature of humanity and defeated every principality and power that ruled over men, making the sin nature predominant. Many other religions are founded on the teachings of a prophet, which is supposed to be a man filled with God in order to speak God's will. The problem is that the sin nature can cause the prophet also to speak out of his human and sinful nature resulting in the texts being mingled with uninspired words. The majority of these religions allow the originating prophet to speak for "God," but deny anyone else to be filled with God's Spirit today. This is why it is dangerous to believe every spiritual book or writing. Now you will ask, "Well, what makes the

Bible different?" The reason the Bible does not embrace every religious teaching is because the 66 books of the Bible were brought together because of their agreement. True doctrine is found when a minimum of two or three texts agree or by the mouth of two or three witnesses. The Holy Spirit does not speak truth through just one mouth, yet anything that is true will line up with Jesus Christ because He is the Way, the Truth and the Life. The Bible specifically leaves out books or texts that contain something spoken that does not agree. By agreement, I do not mean that it does away with the natural account or perspective of the writer, but that the principles found in the truth revealed agree.

For these reasons and many others, many of the clergy inside the walls of the Roman Catholic church found discrepancies in what was practiced, compared to what was written in the Word of God. The public was unable to know about these discrepancies, confined to believe whatever they were told to practice due to the lack of any translation of the Holy Text and the inability for many to read or write. Many of the early church scholars were caught in the faulty systems of religion and were limited to the operations of the hierarchy, which often times was men who were in it for the power instead of for a relationship with God. Over the centuries, hundreds of men were burned at the stake and declared heretics because they asked the Roman Catholic Church to obey the Truth found in the pages of God's Word. God continued to raise up true men of God to speak out against the abuses of authority within the Roman church. During the year of 1517, God had been preparing a German friar and priest by the name of Martin Luther to speak out against the church's use of indulgences to forgive sin. These indulgences were simply certificates, signed by the pope, which forgave sin. A person could buy them with money, therefore money and the pope became the savior and not Jesus Christ. Luther spoke out against these abuses, as well as many others. Out of this came the Protestant movement and the freedom for the Bible to be translated to the common languages of men. This opened the door for God's original intent to have a personal relationship with every man in the heart.

Out of these great reform movements came five principles found in the Bible that deal with salvation. These principles are called the five "solas." This is very interesting because the number five in Hebrew is the letter hey and symbolizes God's acts of grace. The word "solas" is a Latin word that means, "only or alone". The five "solas" are principled statements about how salvation is given to man. The first one is through Scripture alone. Earlier I explained how the various books were brought together to form our Bible, but we need to understand what Scripture is. Scripture is not just mere writing on a tablet or words from a pen. The word for Scripture in Hebrew is, "kathab" which means "a written document with royal enactment and divine authority." The text of God is a royal enactment by our King, whose name is Jesus, He rules and reigns over all the earth. It is also divine decree because it comes from God who is eternal Spirit and created all law that is true and exists. So Scripture text is both law in earth and law in heaven. It is the Truth received from God's Spirit that is God-breathed. It is God speaking to man, through man and man delivering it to us in written form. The written document thereby binds man to be judged in God's court based on what is written and revealed. Salvation comes through Scripture alone.

2 Peter 1:20-21

Knowing this first, that no prophecy of the scripture is of any private interpretation. For the prophecy came not in old time by the will of man: but holy men of God spake as they were moved by the Holy Ghost.

John 1:1 & 14

In the beginning was the Word, and the Word was with God, and the Word was God... And the Word was made flesh, and dwelt among us, (and we beheld his glory, the glory as of the only begotten of the Father,) full of grace and truth.

2 Timothy 3:14-17

But continue thou in the things which thou hast learned and hast been assured of, knowing of whom thou hast learned them; And that from a child thou hast known the holy scriptures, which are able to make thee wise unto salvation through faith which is in Christ Jesus. All scripture is given by inspiration of God, and is profitable for doctrine, for reproof, for correction, for instruction in righteousness: That the man of God may be perfect, thoroughly furnished unto all good works.

2 Peter 2:20

For if after they have escaped the pollutions of the world through the knowledge of the Lord and Saviour Jesus Christ, they are again entangled therein, and overcome, the latter end is worse with them than the beginning.

Romans 15:4

For whatsoever things were written aforetime were written for our learning, that we through patience and comfort of the scriptures might have hope.

In the first chapter of this book, I showed you various texts from the Holy Scripture dealing with faith. It is by watching Biblical examples that we learn who God really is. As you study the Word, you find that the Bible is not just a book of rules, but rather a study of finding out who God is and the lives of different men and women who were in relationship Him. We also see the results of people who left Him out and were used by the enemy. As far as mankind is concerned each one had fault, frailty, and issue, but the ones who continued to seek God and heed His words stayed in relationship with Him and He used their lives. We also see the true nature of God, from His love and law in the Old Testament, to His selfless sacrifice and His restoration of victorious living to man in the New. As we read we find that man's job is to seek His voice and believe. This believing is called faith. Since we talked about it in the first chapter I will move on, but it is the next in the list of the five "solas." Salvation comes by faith alone.

Galatians 3:6-11

Even as Abraham believed God, and it was accounted to him for righteousness. Know ye therefore that they which are of faith, the same are the children of Abraham. And the scripture, foreseeing that God would justify the heathen through faith, preached before the gospel unto Abraham, saying, In thee shall all nations be blessed. So then they which be of faith are blessed with faithful Abraham. For as many as are of the works of the law are under the curse: for it is written, Cursed is every one that continueth not in all things which are written in the book of the law to do them. But that no man is justified by the law in the sight of God, it is evident: for, The just shall live by faith.

Hebrews 11:6

But without faith it is impossible to please him: for he that cometh to God must believe that he is, and that he is a rewarder of them that diligently seek him.

Romans 1:16-18

For I am not ashamed of the gospel of Christ: for it is the power of God unto salvation to every one that believeth; to the Jew first, and also to the Greek. For therein is the righteousness of God revealed from faith to faith: as it is written, the just shall live by faith. For the wrath of God is revealed from heaven against all ungodliness and unrighteousness of men, who hold the truth in unrighteousness.

Salvation is not merely a one time believing. It is literally the process of becoming victorious like Jesus Christ. Our God conquered every enemy we can face, and empowers us by His Spirit to take dominion over personal sin and defeat every foe. This act of Jesus taking the sin of all humanity by becoming a man and paying the price Himself is the greatest act of grace ever given. The earth and the people in it were literally graced with a God who came encountered them face to face. He personally taught the people and worked miracles among people bound in the consequences of sin and pain. This is the ultimate grace for those who believe upon His sacrifice and loving atonement. To those who place their faith in another religion or false god, thereby rejecting God's goodness, there is no grace for them only condemnation (John 3:18-19, Mark 16:16). Salvation is much more than just receiving His atonement it is the desire to be in an intimate relationship where God teaches you to be like Him. While no one deserves such a relationship because of our sinful choices and selfish nature, the Love of God empowers those who believe upon His name to walk in a place that gives them grace to overcome. Grace is number three of the five "solas" and is required to be saved and overcome sin's bondage. Salvation comes by grace alone.

Psalms 84:11-12
For the LORD God is a sun and shield: the LORD will give grace and glory: no good thing will he withhold from them that walk uprightly. O LORD of hosts, blessed is the man that trusteth in thee.

John 1:17

For the law was given by Moses, but grace and truth came by Jesus Christ.

Romans 4:13-16

For the promise, that he should be the heir of the world, was not to Abraham, or to his seed, through the law, but through the righteousness of faith. For if they which are of the law be heirs, faith is made void, and the promise made of none effect: Because the law worketh wrath: for where no law is, there is no transgression. Therefore it is of faith, that it might be by grace; to the end the promise might be sure to all the seed; not to that only which is of the law, but to that also which is of the faith of Abraham; who is the father of us all,

Romans 5:20-21

Moreover the law entered, that the offence might abound. But where sin abounded, grace did much more abound: [21]That as sin hath reigned unto death, even so might grace reign through righteousness unto eternal life by Jesus Christ our Lord.

Since sin is forgiven and paid for by Jesus Christ, all other sources are invalid. They are mere deceptions that lead the follower to be united with a false spirit. These false spirits are the fallen angels that work with Satan to deceive, condemn, and destroy. God never intended for man to be bound in hell (Matthew 25:41, Revelation 12:9), but everlasting fire was made for the devil and his angels. This is why it is important to whom you give your faith. Our faith is not to be placed in man, a religious figure, or deceptive false religions that tend to be works based to attain a place of peace and enlightenment. Our love for Jesus is a true relationship that causes us to place our faith in the one who paid for our sin us to have relationship with us. To place our hope in an object, a man, or doing works to attain relationship with God through man made religion only leads to being joined to another spirit. This is why salvation comes through Jesus Christ alone. This is number four in the five solas.

I Timothy 2:3-8
For this is good and acceptable in the sight of God our Saviour; Who will have all men to be saved, and to come unto the knowledge of the truth. For there is one God, and one mediator between God and men, the man Christ Jesus; Who gave himself a ransom for all, to be testified in due time. Whereunto I am ordained a preacher, and an apostle, (I speak the truth in Christ, and lie not;) a teacher of the Gentiles in faith and verity. I will therefore that men pray every where, lifting up holy hands, without wrath and doubting.

Colossians 1:12-14
Giving thanks unto the Father, which hath made us meet to be partakers of the inheritance of the saints in light: Who hath delivered us from the power of darkness, and hath translated us into the kingdom of his dear Son: In whom we have redemption through his blood, even the forgiveness of sins:

John 14:6-7

I am the way, the truth, and the life: no man cometh unto the Father, but by me. If ye had known me, ye should have known my Father also: and from henceforth ye know him, and have seen him.

This intimate relationship with God himself causes those who follow Jesus to see God at work in every area of their lives. From victory over sin to provision or joy with family and friends, every good gift comes from God and He alone is worthy of all glory. As you come to know, Him you understand that all Truth is His, all goodness is His for He created it all, made it all, and owns it all. He died for every one of us and has a desire to restore the earth to its purpose of being good. This why Christians give glory to God alone. All ability, all talent, all love, and all things good come from God. Man loves to be filled with pride because our sin nature requires personal accolades since the fall. Compared to the love of God at work in your life, all accolades offered by man cannot compare to the relationship you have with the one who gave you all ability. This leads us to the fifth and final "solas." Salvation comes by giving all glory to God alone.

I Peter 4:11

If any man speak, let him speak as the oracles of God; if any man minister, let him do it as of the ability which God giveth: that God in all things may be glorified through Jesus Christ, to whom be praise and dominion for ever and ever. Amen.

Ephesians 3:20-21

Now unto him that is able to do exceeding abundantly above all that we ask or think, according to the power that worketh in us, Unto him be glory in the church by Christ Jesus throughout all ages, world without end. Amen.

Romans 11:33-35

O the depth of the riches both of the wisdom and knowledge of God! how unsearchable are his judgments, and his ways past finding out! For who hath known the mind of the Lord? or who hath been his counsellor? Or who hath first given to him, and it shall be recompensed unto him again? For of him, and through him, and to him, are all things: to whom be glory for ever. Amen.

You may ask why it matters who gets the glory in your life. You must understand that the glory you give is a reflection of the relationship you have with the One who made and owns it all. This is why satan is so jealous because at the end of the day the people who serve him will not rejoice over him or glorify him as those who hold deep relationship with God. Instead the people who are joined to him will curse him, cuss him, and scream at him in pain because he has no power to create anything but anguish in the lives of his followers. In the lake of fire, he will be tormented by his followers who curse his name for eternity, but those who choose Jesus are on a destination that teaches them to glorify His name. Heaven will not be about streets of gold, or gates of pearl, it will be about relationship with a God who is glorified for His goodness day and night. It will be about relationship, adoration, praise, and love. Here on earth our relationship with God is being developed to experience face to face relationship with a God who loves us in return. True salvation is from beginning to eternity and eternal life starts when you accept the Lord.

Revelation 5:12-13
Saying with a loud voice, Worthy is the Lamb that was slain to receive power, and riches, and wisdom, and strength, and honour, and glory, and blessing. And every creature which is in heaven, and on the earth, and under the earth, and such as are in the sea, and all that are in them, heard I saying, Blessing, and honour, and glory, and power, [be] unto him that sitteth upon the throne, and unto the Lamb for ever and ever.

Chapter 4

The Salvation Walk

Soteriology is the word that is used for the study of salvation. The principles learned in this study are not meant to stay written upon the page, but are meant to be walked out and lived from within man's heart. Multitudes of people believe that complete salvation is done simply by saying a prayer or placing their name on the role of a church. They fail to understand that they are making a commitment to God from the heart and giving a verbal commitment with their mouth. The commitment starts in the heart, a heart softened through repentance for sin. When sincere salvation is desired, regeneration and conversion happen within the person's heart. Instead of desiring to live the old nature, they have decided that they are going to go after a relationship with Jesus Christ. With this true heartfelt decision to pursue relationship with God, regeneration happens through the work of the Holy Spirit and that person becomes a new creation, ready to be formed and molded by God.

Titus 3:4-7

But after that the kindness and love of God our Saviour toward man appeared, not by works of righteousness which we have done, but according to his mercy he saved us, by the washing of regeneration, and renewing of the Holy Ghost; which he shed on us abundantly through Jesus Christ our Saviour; that being justified by his grace, we should be made heirs according to the hope of eternal life.

John 3:3

Jesus answered and said unto him, Verily, verily, I say unto thee, Except a man be born again, he cannot see the kingdom of God.

2 Corinthians 5:17

Therefore if any man be in Christ, he is a new creature: old things are passed away; behold, all things are become new.

Galatians 6:15

For in Christ Jesus neither circumcision availeth any thing, nor uncircumcision, but a new creature.

Regeneration and new birth are when the life changing power of the Holy Spirit overwhelms you. It is the place where your desire becomes to love and please the Lord. The old man's desires pass away and a new desire takes their place. This new desire for Jesus causes the individual to move forward in their commitment to God, establishing a fresh and new relationship. Deep feeling and intimate desire for the Savior grow our relationship, moving us to obey the Word of God. Through this obedience, growth takes place and the person changes, taking on more of the image of Jesus Christ. Those who have truly received salvation have a burning desire to learn the ways of God. They desire to know God and His ways of righteousness. They are very willing to make the commitment. True conversion is not just a five minute event, it is a place where relationship happens and the person longs to know God through the Holy Spirit and the Word. This relationship is so real and powerful that it lasts beyond a lifetime. Scripture gives us the analogy of marriage like unto Christ and His Church. His Church is not a building, but rather is the people. Marriage is an act of commitment held between two individuals. These two become one through the solemn act of commitment and relationship. A true marriage lasts "till death do us part" after the couple take the vows. Our relationship with Jesus is eternal because He defeated death and there will be no parting. To say the prayer and then return to your old way is like a marriage that never happened. No spouse would dare say he had a marriage if his wife was with another man five minutes after they made their vows. In fact, I am sure that marriage would be annulled. It would be as if it never existed. There have been many people who have come to the front of a church said the prayer of salvation with little or no heartfelt commitment. They think they have salvation, but fail to understand that they made a vow of commitment to God. This vow requires a relationship by walking with God, talking with God and desiring to submit to His authority. It requires a true love for God Himself.

In our day, with so many different versions of salvation, people tend to have a problem understanding what is being asked when posed the question "Are you saved?" Most of time individuals answer yes, but if you probe a little further you will find that many have little or no relationship with God. They are referring to a time and place they filled out a card, said the prayer, were baptized into a church, or heard the preacher say they got "saved." When you ask "How is your relationship with God?" a look of fear comes over their face. Excuses tend to follow and explanations about how they have a busy life. It is not the preacher, the prayer, or the baptism that is going to save you. Your salvation is totally dependent on your relationship with God. Only you know where your relationship is currently. It is the Holy Spirit's job to tell you that you are right with God and it is your job to know that you are constantly ready to meet the Lord and stand before Him.

Romans 8:15-17
For ye have not received the spirit of bondage again to fear; but ye have received the Spirit of adoption, whereby we cry, Abba, Father. The Spirit itself beareth witness with our spirit, that we are the children of God: And if children, then heirs; heirs of God, and joint-heirs with Christ; if so be that we suffer with him, that we may be also glorified together.

2 Corinthians 1:22

Who hath also sealed us, and given the earnest of the Spirit in our hearts.

Ephesians 1:13-14

In whom ye also trusted, after that ye heard the word of truth, the gospel of your salvation: in whom also after that ye believed, ye were sealed with that Holy Spirit of promise, which is the earnest of our inheritance until the redemption of the purchased possession, unto the praise of his glory.

Our relationship with God is so powerful that His work in our lives should be top priority on our list. It is not that we operate in a spirit of paranoia or fear concerning our relationship with God. It is that we are in a constant state of desiring Him and loving anything He wants to teach us. Our heart's desire is to seek Him and honor Him in all our ways. Inevitably, we will make mistakes. But instead of running away in fear, we run to God. True salvation knows God has saved you from your past sin, He is saving you from your current sin, and He will save you in the future. It is knowing that by honoring this One relationship above all others, God is going to cause you to overcome. The salvation of Jesus Christ is found in this relationship that just keeps giving and giving until you are so overcome with His love you can't help but want to be like Him. Every day you find you are hungry for more of the Word and the Spirit simply because it holds all the answers and healing needed to face every issue in your life. This is what makes our salvation so intimate and personal.

Philippians 2:12-16

Wherefore, my beloved, as ye have always obeyed, not as in my presence only, but now much more in my absence, work out your own salvation with fear and trembling. For it is God which worketh in you both to will and to do of his good pleasure. Do all things without murmurings and disputings: That ye may be blameless and harmless, the sons of God, without rebuke, in the midst of a crooked and perverse nation, among whom ye shine as lights in the world; Holding forth the word of life; that I may rejoice in the day of Christ, that I have not run in vain, neither laboured in vain.

It is God's good pleasure to work out every situation you will face, if you will simply honor Him by seeking and obeying His Word of life. Salvation is intimate, personal, and individual because God knows exactly what each man will face in the area of sin. To God, all sin is the same and when you break one law, you break them all. Yet he has a desire to show you how to overcome every enemy you face. With each issue, you must obey Him with the correct heart attitude and response. Your salvation is one you work out within yourself as you evaluate your heart response about obeying God. Paul is saying to the Philippians to respond correctly to God even when he is nowhere around. True salvation is lived whether the preacher is present or not. When you break down the words fear and trembling in the Greek, you see the heart of the individual who is saved. It can be translated, "Work out your own salvation with reverence for Jesus as a husband, as one who does not trust their own ability to meet all the requirements, but does their best to fulfill their duty." This is a picture of a relationship where you give your all and God takes care of your area of weakness. This relationship is one of growth, victory, and love, empowering us to depend more on God with every obstacle causing us to press deeper into His Spirit until we become like Him. Our salvation is a relationship that says, "I was saved, I am being saved, and I shall be saved!" True salvation is growing and depending on God more every day and loving every minute of it. Those who follow through all the way to the end have nothing to fear. The idea is to love God all the way through, no matter what. Let's look at a few texts.

Matthew 10:21-22
And the brother shall deliver up the brother to death, and the father the child: and the children shall rise up against their parents, and cause them to be put to death. And ye shall be hated of all men for my name's sake: but he that endureth to the end shall be saved.

Matthew 24:10-13
And then shall many be offended, and shall betray one another, and shall hate one another. And many false prophets shall rise, and shall deceive many. And because iniquity shall abound, the love of many shall wax cold. But he that shall endure unto the end, the same shall be saved.

No matter how men around us change or how the world wants to mistreat us based on our relationship with Jesus, we must be prepared to live our relationship with Jesus to the end. There will be many who start well but don't finish well. Satan has a desire to detour our relationship with God. If he can get you off course, he knows you will develop a relationship with something else. Our salvation with Christ is past, present and future. It is a relationship that will endure if we will just give ourselves over to Him. Our salvation cannot be in the past, for God is a present help in the time of need. We have to be determined to serve God in our future. Some people will not get to live with God for eternity, because He will not force you to go to a place you will not love. If you don't love God, His Spirit or His Word here on earth, why would He have you spend eternity with Him? The word for endure in Greek is "hypomeno." It means to not recede in commitment, or flee in the face of hardship or persecution. The word end is "telos" which means to sell out for a definite finishing point or goal. Both of these words tell the story of those who are truly saved. They will not stop, no matter what comes. They will follow Jesus until they become just like Him and spend eternity with Him. This relationship with Christ is so powerful that it is right to treat it with the greatest reverence, respect, and value.

So many of us just throw the word "saved" around in a light manner instead of valuing the relationship that has been given to us. The apostles understood that serving God was a way of life. It was the complete work that should be pursued. The complete work was to please the Lord at every turn, knowing that each day would require a personal giving over to do God's will. Peter demonstrates this level of obedience when dealing with what would be required of the Gentile believers in Acts 15:8-11. He says "And God, which knoweth the hearts, bare them witness, giving them the Holy Ghost, even as he did unto us; And put no difference between us and them, purifying their hearts by faith. Now therefore why tempt ye God, to put a yoke upon the neck of the disciples, which neither our fathers nor we were able to bear? But we believe that through the grace of the Lord Jesus Christ we shall be saved, even as they." You notice that Peter did not declare personal salvation for all of the apostles and elders, but instead used the statement, "we shall be saved." This insinuates that even they had not reached the ultimate finishing work of salvation. I believe Paul understood this principle when he said this in 1 Corinthians 9:27; "But I keep under my body, and bring it into subjection: lest that by any means, when I have preached to others, I myself should be a castaway." Our relationship with God is a lifelong pursuit of His voice, His love, and His will.

Many people want to limit the experience of salvation to one certain text or one certain work or action to receive it. There are many texts that speak about what is required and we must consider them all. We also need to look into the true meanings of the words spoken. Those who are not living a relationship with Jesus, tend to want to perform certain texts just to escape hell. I have heard many people say, "if you call out the name of Jesus you will be saved." They think the act itself saves you because that is what the text states. If this is the case every person who said Jesus Christ as a cuss word would be qualified to enter into the pearly gates.

Acts 2:21
And it shall come to pass, that whosoever shall call on the name of the Lord shall be saved.

Romans 10:13
For whosoever shall call upon the name of the Lord shall be saved.

At first glance, it looks like you cry out and you are saved. In actuality, the Greek translation should read, "Anyone who wants to take the name and come to know God's excellences, commands, pleasures, authority and deeds, will receive God as helper, witness and judge, and shall be saved." To call out for God's name is to desire to know Him intimately. It is a call that asks His name to come upon you so that you can bear His image and His way of being. Again, we see a relational work that desires to be like God.

Another group of texts that need to be addressed is the group that adds the work of baptism. While I do not believe the water in the tank saves you, I do believe that anyone who has had conversion will desire to be baptized. The truth is, someone who has been saved will want to obey everything in God's Book. Everything that God asks of us has a purpose and is based in a principled understanding. In many cases, people are rushed to the water without ever understanding the meaning behind it. Countless people have argued over whether the act of baptism saves you, but what they fail to realize is that this moment is a notification to the physical body that it is going to die to sin and arise to new life (Romans 6:3-4, Colossians 2:11-12). Without true heart change of the individual, this moment can be nothing more for them than taking a bath. All of these moments represent the true inward change that is desired by the individual and should be treated with great dignity and respect. Every aspect of salvation should be understood by the individual who desires relationship with Christ. We should not rush people into a relationship they may not desire, just because we want them to. This relationship with Jesus Christ is real and has to be real in the heart of the one receiving it. It is not simply about the work of baptism; all outward works must first be understood and received with Jesus being in the center of the heart.

Matthew 16:15
And he said unto them, Go ye into all the world, and preach the gospel to every creature. He that believeth and is baptized shall be saved; but he that believeth not shall be damned.

Acts 2:41
Then they that gladly received his word were baptized.

Acts 8:36-37

And as they went on their way, they came unto a certain water: and the eunuch said, See, here is water; what doth hinder me to be baptized? And Philip said, If thou believest with all thine heart, thou mayest. And he answered and said, I believe that Jesus Christ is the Son of God.

1 Corinthians 1:17-18

For Christ sent me not to baptize, but to preach the gospel: not with wisdom of words, lest the cross of Christ should be made of none effect. For the preaching of the cross is to them that perish foolishness; but unto us which are saved it is the power of God.

We see that the message of the Gospel and the preaching of the cross is the central theme to understanding salvation and desiring a relationship with God. This text also takes us to another issue which needs to be addressed concerning salvation. Earlier, we made the declaration that; "I was saved from my past sin, I am being saved from my present sin, and shall be saved." This declaration is one that causes us to overcome every obstacle by staying in intimate relationship with God. One of the main reasons people think that salvation is limited to the moment we first believe is because of texts like the one in 1 Corinthians above. It says; "to us which are saved." To have correct verb tense it should say; "to us which are being saved." This is a verb in present tense which requires this to be a present action. Other texts that have the same tense issue are

Romans 8:24, I Corinthians 15:2, 2 Corinthians 2:15, and Ephesians 2:5. This does not do away with our initial experience of our old sins being washed away. The place of regeneration is a real and powerful introduction to Jesus Christ. Paul deals with this in Titus 3:4-5, where he says this to Titus: "But after that the kindness and love of God our Saviour toward man appeared, not by works of righteousness which we have done, but according to His mercy He saved us, by the washing of regeneration, and renewing of the Holy Ghost." Our salvation walk does not end with initial introduction to Christ; rather, it just begins. As we develop our relationship, we go deeper into the things of God and find out that our relationship saves us in the present as well. Understanding that our salvation is past, present and future brings us to other texts that many people fail to understand, especially if they think the initial introduction is the end of their salvation. Let's look at these texts.

Romans 13:11-14

And that, knowing the time, that now it is high time to awake out of sleep: for now [is] our salvation nearer than when we believed. The night is far spent, the day is at hand: let us therefore cast off the works of darkness, and let us put on the armour of light. Let us walk honestly, as in the day; not in rioting and drunkenness, not in chambering and wantonness, not in strife and envying. But put ye on the Lord Jesus Christ, and make not provision for the flesh, to fulfil the lusts thereof.

2 Timothy 4:18

And the Lord shall deliver me from every evil work, and will preserve (save) me unto his heavenly kingdom: to whom be glory for ever and ever. Amen.

1 Peter 1:7-9

That the trial of your faith, being much more precious than of gold that perisheth, though it be tried with fire, might be found unto praise and honour and glory at the appearing of Jesus Christ: Whom having not seen, ye love; in whom, though now ye see him not, yet believing, ye rejoice with joy unspeakable and full of glory: Receiving the end of your faith, even the salvation of your souls.

All three of these texts are speaking of the final completion of the ongoing salvation experience in your life. We must understand that every day we spend in relationship with Jesus Christ is another day we are given to become more like Him. The complete work of salvation is to "put on Christ" through every moment of struggle in this life. We are being delivered from every evil work and entering into a greater understanding of His heavenly kingdom. While the verse in 2 Timothy says, "preserve," it is the word "sozo" in Greek, which is the same word often used for, "save, being saved, and shall be saved." As we walk with Jesus, His Holy Spirit is leading and guiding us into all Truth (John 16:13). It is impossible to come into relationship with Jesus and not grow in the things of God. The only way for you to stay stagnant is for you to work at damaging your relationship with Jesus yourself, or by you pretending you have relationship with Him when you really don't. I need to say it again. It is impossible to have a relationship with Jesus and not grow. When you spend time with Him you will bring forth the fruit of His Spirit, understand more of the Word, and place more faith in Him each day as your relationship grows. This is why the Scripture says this in Romans 1:17: "For therein is the righteousness of God revealed from faith to faith: as it is written, the just shall live by faith." God is revealing His right way of living, thinking and being to us so that we increase in Him and bear His image. Our relationship with Jesus is one that is to be desired. We must seek the Lord and expect Him to help us over come every obstacle we face. By following and believing in Jesus Christ we find that our faith increases.

Hebrews 11:6
But without faith it is impossible to please him: for he that cometh to God must believe that he is, and that he is a rewarder of them that diligently seek him.

Colossians 1:23
If ye continue in the faith grounded and settled, and be not moved away from the hope of the gospel, which ye have heard, and which was preached to every creature which is under heaven; whereof I Paul am made a minister;

Our salvation is not just based in a one-time prayer, but a constant placing of our hope in the victorious nature of Jesus Christ. Our faith gives us hope that every struggle can be defeated, and every sin overcome simply by keeping our relationship right with Jesus. We don't place our hope in the leader, the church, the prayer, or even a certain work, we place our hope in Jesus Christ who is able to teach, and grow, and mature us in the knowledge of the Gospel as we follow Him. Jesus has wrought for us a great salvation and a wonderful plan. If we follow Him, we know Him more, experience His goodness and live His freedom by breaking the chains of sin's bondage. He gives us hope and we give Him all the glory. Nothing can compare to this relationship with Jesus Christ. Our salvation is fashioned in faith and hope, knowing everything Jesus has done for us. Our relationship will cause us to bear the image of an overcomer because that is who He is. As we acknowledge His Word and know Him more, we place our hope in His Truth and this brings true life. We really go from glory to glory. I was saved from my past sin, I am being saved from my present sin, and I shall be saved in the future, if I will just keep following Him and seeking His way. He doesn't just deliver me from sin. He teaches me his Word and causes me to rule and reign over sin by His Spirit that comes to set me free. That is the power of a relationship with Jesus Christ.

Romans 8:24-28

For we are saved by hope: but hope that is seen is not hope: for what a man seeth, why doth he yet hope for? But if we hope for that we see not, then do we with patience wait for it. Likewise the Spirit also helpeth our infirmities: for we know not what we should pray for as we ought: but the Spirit itself maketh intercession for us with groanings which cannot be uttered. And he that searcheth the hearts knoweth what is the mind of the Spirit, because he maketh intercession for the saints according to the will of God. And we know that all things work together for good to them that love God, to them who are the called according to his purpose.

2 Corinthians 3:17-18

Now the Lord is that Spirit: and where the Spirit of the Lord is, there is liberty. But we all, with open face beholding as in a glass the glory of the Lord, are changed into the same image from glory to glory, even as by the Spirit of the Lord.

Chapter 5

The Life of the Just

The Salvation walk is continuous and glorious. It is taken one step at a time into a marvelous and miraculous work where God and man come into the state of restored union. The restored union with God through believing upon Jesus Christ sets us free from sin and unlocks powerful keys (Luke 11:52, Matthew 19:16, Revelation 1:18) that transform our lives. Salvation opens us up to every opportunity of restoration listed in the Word. Once you believe upon the Lord Jesus Christ, accept His atoning work, and have a sincere desire to yield to His Lordship, you need to know the next key in the total walk of salvation. This is found in a word called justification. This key cannot be attained by man through his own means due to the sin nature itself. Jesus himself lived a sinless life and He alone bears the right to all things in the earth, beneath the earth, and in heaven. By living a sinless and perfect life, and fulfilling all the law, the rights are His alone. Instead of using His rights to fulfill the selfish nature of the flesh, He allowed the sin nature in other men to crucify His flesh in order to restore mankind back to the Spirit of God. The Spirit of God restores us back to God's goodness giving us the right to receive every promise inside of God's Word.

Since the fall of Adam man, has lacked the ability to completely access all that God has promised. To receive every benefit meant for mankind in the earth, man must meet the total requirement of being just. While we see men through the Bible text that followed after God and reaped a certain understanding or promise, we find that while they succeeded in one area they failed in another. This is the problem with the nature of the flesh. According to the law, we are only justified to receive what is rightfully due you. This means that we have pay coming to us for doing what right, and penalty is coming to us for our wrong. The word just in the Hebrew is "tsaddiyq." It means to do what is lawful, correct or right. Under this definition, we find that there is no man who is just in all areas of life.

Ezekiel 18:5-9

But if a man be just, and do that which is lawful and right, And hath not eaten upon the mountains, neither hath lifted up his eyes to the idols of the house of Israel, neither hath defiled his neighbour's wife, neither hath come near to a menstruous woman, And hath not oppressed any, but hath restored to the debtor his pledge, hath spoiled none by violence, hath given his bread to the hungry, and hath covered the naked with a garment; He that hath not given forth upon usury, neither hath taken any increase, that hath withdrawn his hand from iniquity, hath executed true judgment between man and man, Hath walked in my statutes, and hath kept my judgments, to deal truly; he is just, he shall surely live, saith the Lord GOD.

This text in Ezekiel gives us a verbal outline of what it is for someone to be just. After carefully looking over its text, I am sure you find no human who has met all of these requirements. Even the greatest of the patriarchs fail to meet this list. Ecclesiastes 7:20 says, "For there is not a just man upon earth, that doeth good, and sinneth not." This is why the Old Testament law requires payment for sin, either through the giving of an animal, an offering, or something of monetary value. These sacrifices were meant to show God that man still had a heart to do right. It was meant as a way to bring man back to God so man could continue to be directed by God through His Word and Spirit. The problem is that, no matter what outward work God required, man still refused relationship with God and continued to be directed by their own wicked heart. The works failed to qualify a return to God. Instead man just used the payment as a way to keep right on sinning. The law failed because the people just gave God the sacrifice without making the true sacrifice of following God in an intimate relationship. Instead of qualifying man simply by law, God turned to looking at the heart (1 Samuel 16:7, 1 Chronicles 28:9.2 Chronicles 16:9). God is all about the relationship. Even though there were no just men in the earth, God formed relationship with the patriarchs because of their heart and their willingness to follow Him by faith. Those who followed from the heart became known as just men, but even they had a habit of falling.

Proverbs 24:26

For a just man falleth seven times, and riseth up again: but the wicked shall fall into mischief.

Proverbs 4:11-19

I have taught thee in the way of wisdom; I have led thee in right paths. When thou goest, thy steps shall not be straitened; and when thou runnest, thou shalt not stumble. Take fast hold of instruction; let her not go: keep her; for she is thy life. Enter not into the path of the wicked, and go not in the way of evil men. Avoid it, pass not by it, turn from it, and pass away. For they sleep not, except they have done mischief; and their sleep is taken away, unless they cause some to fall. For they eat the bread of wickedness, and drink the wine of violence. But the path of the just is as the shining light, that shineth more and more unto the perfect day. The way of the wicked is as darkness: they know not at what they stumble.

Psalms 7:8-11

The LORD shall judge the people: judge me, O LORD, according to my righteousness, and according to mine integrity that is in me.Oh let the wickedness of the wicked come to an end; but establish the just: for the righteous God trieth the hearts and reins. My defence is of God, which saveth the upright in heart. God judgeth the righteous, and God is angry with the wicked every day.

The heart of the man desiring to be just is far different than that of the wicked. Instead of being taught by God, the wicked man wants to do things his own way. The just man constantly seeks the way of the Lord, desiring His wisdom with all of his heart. No matter how much the justified heart desired God, man remained unable to bear God's nature and image. His sin disqualified him even though he desired God. It was a constant effort to keep his heart in line with God's will. The sin nature not only lives in the flesh of man, but it also lives in the heart. The Greek word for just is "dikaios." It further defines a just man as "him whose way of thinking, feeling, and acting is wholly conformed to the will of God, and therefore needs no rectification of the heart, making one approved and acceptable to God." When you look at this definition it further reveals the need for man to learn to yield to God's righteous Word. Through the Word we know what is right, but this still brings us to feelings of condemnation because the sin nature always condemns us because of our mistakes. Man may attempt to obey God, but inevitably they will fail without the empowerment of the Spirit. Even the man with the most pure intent and upright heart will fail without correction from the Holy Spirit. The man desiring to cleanse his way must learn to bring God His heart and let it be judged. Jeremiah 17:9 says, "The heart is deceitful above all things, and desperately wicked: who can know it? I the LORD search the heart, I try the reins, even to give every man according to his ways, and according to the fruit of his doings." This is why letting God judge our hearts is so important. It reveals wrong thoughts, wrong motives, and wrong choices being made. Even when the individual desires to do God's will, the man himself will have weakness and fault and the result will be some sort of sin. The man desiring God's righteousness will allow the Lord to search him so he can find his way. This is why sin forgiveness and the blood of Jesus is imperitive. It keeps man in right relationship with God while the man seeks direction and correction from God to give God His will. The salvation that Jesus obtained for us causes those who believe in Jesus Christ to be able to access all the benefits God has for them even though they fail.

Acts 13:38

Be it known unto you therefore, men and brethren, that through this man is preached unto you the forgiveness of sins: And by him all that believe are justified from all things, from which ye could not be justified by the law of Moses.

I Peter 3:18

For Christ also hath once suffered for sins, the just for the unjust, that he might bring us to God, being put to death in the flesh, but quickened by the Spirit:

The ultimate restoration that could happen for man came through Jesus Christ. The blood of Jesus washes man clean so he can be filled with the Holy Spirit to be taught and developed by God. This is why Jesus is sinless and He alone is just. His sin redemption not only restores humanity, but it justifies each one of us to walk into the promises of God. Our relationship with Jesus redeems us from the curse of the law and brings us into right standing with God. When you are justified by Christ you not only qualify for the promise, you are also justified to live the Word of God. This relationship with Christ is not only going to walk you into the promises, it is going to teach you to rule and reign with Christ.

Through the work of the Holy Spirit you will be taught to live the whole Word. An analogy I would like to use is one that involves the word processing program on your computer. When you type a document you are given the option of right alignment, left alignment, center, or justify. When you click the justify button, it causes the words to spread across the whole margin. When visualized, this gives us a visual demonstration of justification concerning the Word. When you are walking in salvation, you are qualified to receive the whole Bible cover to cover. All of the Word is opened to you, and the Holy Spirit is going to direct and guide you into it as you grow in relationship and learn to obey and fulfill God's will, God's way. As you yield to the Holy Spirit, you will find that God will not withhold any good thing from you. You qualify for every promise by entering into the salvation walk with Jesus Christ. All you have to do is release your faith in the Total Promise of God. Every time you believe the Word of God over your old nature, you are made righteous and are released to obey the Word from faith to faith and glory to glory. This is what it means for the just to live by faith. It is by believing Jesus through His Word that you grow into the image of Christ. As the body of Christ, we are still on the earth fulfilling the will of the Father and Jesus is alive within each of us.

Romans 1:16-18

For I am not ashamed of the gospel of Christ: for it is the power of God unto salvation to every one that believeth; to the Jew first, and also to the Greek. For therein is the righteousness of God revealed from faith to faith: as it is written, The just shall live by faith. For the wrath of God is revealed from heaven against all ungodliness and unrighteousness of men, who hold the truth in unrighteousness; Because that which may be known of God is manifest in them; for God hath showed it unto them.

Romans 3:21-26

But now the righteousness of God without the law is manifested, being witnessed by the law and the prophets;Even the righteousness of God which is by faith of Jesus Christ unto all and upon all them that believe: for there is no difference: For all have sinned, and come short of the glory of God;Being justified freely by his grace through the redemption that is in Christ Jesus: Whom God hath set forth to be a propitiation through faith in his blood, to declare his righteousness for the remission of sins that are past, through the forbearance of God; To declare, I say, at this time his righteousness: that he might be just, and the justifier of him which believeth in Jesus.

By being washed in the blood of Jesus, you restore your relationship with God. You have been washed to return to the walk of the Holy Spirit. Jesus has cleansed you and made you fit to be filled with the precious Holy Spirit so He can lead and guide you into all Truth. The Holy Spirit is so powerful that He caused the Gentiles to obey the principles of God from their heart without them knowing the written law which contained the principles. This demonstration is given to us in Romans 2:13-16 it says "For not the hearers of the law are just before God, but the doers of the law shall be justified. For when the Gentiles, which have not the law, do by nature the things contained in the law, these, having not the law, are a law unto themselves: Which show the work of the law written in their hearts, their conscience also bearing witness, and their thoughts the mean while accusing or else excusing one another; In the day when God shall judge the secrets of men by Jesus Christ according to my gospel." This powerful text reveals that your relationship with God can become so intimate that He himself will justify you and teach you all things. This does not exclude the Word, but rather the Word and the Spirit agree, causing the Word not to be something performed off the page, but by heart relationship instead. A genuine relationship with Jesus through the work of the Holy Spirit is going to purify you and cause you to live the very Word of God. The Word of God becomes a road map leading humanity to God to fulfill God's will on the earth. The first step in this process is for you to know that you are justified to receive, live, and grow into the whole Word of God. Don't let any person or demonic spirit convince you otherwise. Go after God and expect Him to teach you. He will teach you through His Word, and by His Spirit. You will find Him speaking to you from the mouths of His fivefold leaders (Ephesians 4), through relationships with people within the body of Christ, in your everyday walk with

Jesus Christ and intimately by a still small voice. The first relationship key is understanding you are not disqualified, you are just if your heart longs after Him and you are committed to Him by relationship.

I Corinthians 6:9-11

Know ye not that the unrighteous shall not inherit the kingdom of God? Be not deceived: neither fornicators, nor idolaters, nor adulterers, nor effeminate, nor abusers of themselves with mankind, Nor thieves, nor covetous, nor drunkards, nor revilers, nor extortioners, shall inherit the kingdom of God. And such were some of you: but ye are washed, but ye are sanctified, but ye are justified in the name of the Lord Jesus, and by the Spirit of our God.

Chapter 6

True Grace

To understand grace is to gain knowledge of one of the most intricate keys used to unlock growth in your walk of salvation. Like your salvation relationship, you need to be aware that grace given by God is a beautiful gift for those longing to grow and move forward in God's kingdom. It has nothing to do with God leaving you in your hurt and sin, but has everything to do with the believer becoming victorious and walking as an overcomer. The various religious misinterpretations have taken this key of victory and turned it into nothing more than God allowing men to indulge their sin nature and still participate with His divine nature after they are through. This ideal causes great confusion in the church because leaders assign people to God who have no desire to take on His nature or to bear His image. Teaching grace this way stops the purpose of God's grace and essentially leaves people in slavery to sin and its bondage.

The delivering power of salvation causes the new creature to hate the sin nature and desire to put on the new man. This desire to be like Jesus Christ is the core desire in a relationship with God. It is this cry of heart that empowers the believer to go towards the mark and standard of Jesus Christ. If Christ is the goal or standard to be met, then affirming people who love their sin nature to keep sinning is not going to help them reach the goal. This is why a true understanding of Biblical grace is so crucial to those walking in salvation. Grace is given to take you somewhere; it is a key in your relationship with God that keeps you in relationship with Him while He empowers you to overcome individual weakness and personal struggle. In the Word of God, you find the word "grace" occurring in several different contexts. First is in the context of Jesus Christ sent to earth and gracing humanity with his life so they can be saved. If the individual fails to believe upon Jesus Christ and rejects such a great offer of salvation, then the only thing left is condemnation, and pain in this life, with eternal judgment to follow. Another context is God gracing men with individual gifts and callings. When the gifts and calling are used according to God's will, God graces the individual to further His kingdom work and accomplish His purposes. The primary way that the word grace is used is in the area of believers being freed from sin and released into righteousness.

The meaning of the Greek word "charis" is one with many contextual meanings: it is unmerited favor, it is God's power to keep and strengthen, and it is grace that increases people with Christian faith, knowledge and affection, bringing them to the exercise of the Christian virtues. For those walking in salvation, grace is God's power to overcome sin by allowing God to teach and sustain them through the process. A physical analogy can be found in the context of a mortgage payment. The mortgage payment was due on the first of the month, but you were given a grace period that allowed you to wait to pay it until the fifteenth. You were given time to gather the funds without accruing a penalty. This is a picture of God's grace. As a believer, God grants you time to be taught how to overcome. Not only does He give you time to learn, but He also empowers you and sustains you while you go through the process. True grace is given to the justified believer to help with the processes of righteousness, sanctification and holiness.

Psalms 84:11-12
For the LORD God is a sun and shield: the LORD will give grace and glory: no good thing will he withhold from them that walk uprightly. O LORD of hosts, blessed is the man that trusteth in thee.

In our salvation walk, grace is directly connected with our ability to believe God's Word and to walk in the Truth. This principle is exemplified by our Savior Jesus Christ. When it came to God staring humanity in the face, He took on the nature of the flesh. He was graced by God through the power of the Spirit to rule over the flesh. This came by making the flesh acknowledge the Truth and yield to the power of the Spirit. What the law could not do with the sin nature of man, God performed by becoming the Word and graced the flesh with the power of the Spirit. It was the empowerment of the Spirit that ruled over the sin nature, and it was obedience to the Word that kept the body sinless. God's sinless sacrifice would open the door to Spiritual empowerment which would help mankind live what is right. Grace and Truth are so intricately connected that both are required to walk in the Spirit. To have a relationship with God, we must understand His Spirit requires both (Hebrews 10:29, John 16:13). We cannot walk in Christ without expecting God to tell us the Truth and grace us with the empowering work of His Spirit so we can live it. John 1:14-17 says, "And the Word was made flesh, and dwelt among us, (and we beheld his glory, the glory as of the only begotten of the Father,) full of grace and truth. John bare witness of him, and cried, saying, this was he of whom I spake, He that cometh after me is preferred before me: for he was before me. And of his fulness have all we received, and grace for grace. For the law was given by Moses, but grace and truth came by Jesus Christ." For us to be the body of Christ, we must be walking epistles that are read by men. We must be the walking Word. There is no way for this to be accomplished without the desire to be full of grace and Truth. Receiving a relationship with Jesus transforms us inwardly, but walking in the Spirit and receiving the Truth of the Word transforms us outwardly. This mighty work of the Spirit causes the flesh to give way to the will of God. The grace of God that came as the form of a man and died for us on Calvary, empowers us to receive the grace to live the Truth. It is grace for grace. God graced us to be empowered to walk as He walked and live as He lived. This powerful text reveals God's heart towards us and allows us to reach out in faith to receive this ultimate transformation.

Romans 5:18-21

Therefore as by the offence of one judgment came upon all men to condemnation; even so by the righteousness of one the free gift came upon all men unto justification of life. For as by one man's disobedience many were made sinners, so by the obedience of one shall many be made righteous. Moreover the law entered, that the offence might abound. But where sin abounded, grace did much more abound: That as sin hath reigned unto death, even so might grace reign through righteousness unto eternal life by Jesus Christ our Lord.

The grace of Jesus Christ abounded over every sin. You must let grace reign in your life through righteousness unto eternal life. Righteousness is the state of believing what is right. It is the state of receiving the Truth. The Bible clearly states that Abraham believed God and it was counted unto him as righteousness (Romans 4:3, Galatians 3:6, James 2:23). Every time you believe the Word of God over your own weakness and fleshly desire, you are empowered and graced by the Holy Spirit to reach the goal. With every obstacle, the Holy Spirit comes to teach you to overcome. The time needed to learn the principles and overcome is the grace of God at work in your life. God does not instantly leave you when you fail, but He desires for you to hear the Truth. As you hear the Truth, He empowers you even greater until you reach the goal, overcome the sin, and walk in victory.

Titus 2:11-14

For the grace of God that bringeth salvation hath appeared to all men, Teaching us that, denying ungodliness and worldly lusts, we should live soberly, righteously, and godly, in this present world; Looking for that blessed hope, and the glorious appearing of the great God and our Saviour Jesus Christ; Who gave himself for us, that he might redeem us from all iniquity, and purify unto himself a peculiar people, zealous of good works.

Romans 6:12-18

Let not sin therefore reign in your mortal body, that ye should obey it in the lusts thereof. Neither yield ye your members as instruments of unrighteousness unto sin: but yield yourselves unto God, as those that are alive from the dead, and your members as instruments of righteousness unto God. For sin shall not have dominion over you: for ye are not under the law, but under grace. What then? Shall we sin, because we are not under the law, but under grace? God forbid. Know ye not, that to whom ye yield yourselves servants to obey, his servants ye are to whom ye obey; whether of sin unto death, or of obedience unto righteousness? But God be thanked, that ye were the servants of sin, but ye have obeyed from the heart that form of doctrine which was delivered you. Being then made free from sin, ye became the servants of righteousness. I speak after the manner of men because of the infirmity of your flesh: for as ye have yielded your members servants to uncleanness and to iniquity unto iniquity; even so now yield your members servants to righteousness unto holiness.

Having knowledge of sin does not give us the ability to overcome it. It takes a work of the Holy Spirit, who convicts of sin and comes against the flesh. The time given to overcome sin is grace given to the justified. The grace of God comes to teach us. It causes us to look for Jesus Christ to appear. Not only does the text in Titus imply God's bodily return, but it also implies God appearing in us; that we would be the bearers of His image in the earth, the actual body of Jesus Christ. Grace has come so that sin will not have dominion over us. Instead, Jesus takes dominion over the sin in our lives and teaches us to reign with Him. We are called to be set free from sin. Jesus has taken all dominion and is reigning in our lives. He is taking His rightful place, teaching us to follow Him into the Spirit, defeating the sin nature in the flesh. Our physical bodies are not called to serve sin, but rather to serve righteousness. We are called to walk with God to the point we become more than conquerors through Him that loved us. This is the "faith to faith and glory to glory." In our salvation walk, we should be constantly moving forward - growing in Christ. In this life, we face issue after issue, but with Jesus on our side we will not suffer defeat. Our relationship with God is a personal one; He knows exactly how long it will take to overcome each issue. As we walk with God, He will bring up each obstacle and teach us to overcome it. Some issues will take longer to overcome than others, but the idea is to follow Jesus to the point of victory. We cannot recede in faith or commitment to God; we must expect God and trust His timing. This is the value of our relationship with God. He knows each of us personally, and as long as we follow Him, He will lead us to the land of promise.

It is Christ in us, the hope of glory. This intimate relationship with God, from the heart, is going to make us righteous as we yield to His grace and His Truth.

Galatians 2:20-21
I am crucified with Christ: nevertheless I live; yet not I, but Christ liveth in me: and the life which I now live in the flesh I live by the faith of the Son of God, who loved me, and gave himself for me. I do not frustrate the grace of God: for if righteousness come by the law, then Christ is dead in vain.

Hebrews 12:27-29
And this word, Yet once more, signifieth the removing of those things that are shaken, as of things that are made, that those things which cannot be shaken may remain. Wherefore we receiving a kingdom which cannot be moved, let us have grace, whereby we may serve God acceptably with reverence and godly fear: For our God is a consuming fire.

This relationship of grace given to you by God is calling you to the place of learning to yield to God's Truth and experience the overcoming power of His Spirit. The key of God's transforming grace is to let God's Word be final in every area of your life by letting the Holy Spirit lead you to face every temptation. Stay in relationship with Jesus Christ and He will lead you to victory. One victory gives way to another, until the person you were is not who you are. The inward work of relationship with God causes a change in your life that is truly glorious. Never be impatient, but face each battle with a strength and willingness to learn from God and watch Him shake off every issue that holds you back.

2 Peter 1:2-4
Grace and peace be multiplied unto you through the knowledge of God, and of Jesus our Lord, According as his divine power hath given unto us all things that pertain unto life and godliness, through the knowledge of him that hath called us to glory and virtue: Whereby are given unto us exceeding great and precious promises: that by these ye might be partakers of the divine nature, having escaped the corruption that is in the world through lust.

1 Corinthians 15:49
And as we have borne the image of the earthy, we shall also bear the image of the heavenly.

Chapter 7

The Day of the Saints

Our salvation and relationship with God is not just designed to keep us from going to hell. The Word of God is at work to save us and fulfill God's original purposes in the earth. When you limit salvation to a simple prayer, you limit the ability of the individual to understand that God has a specific purpose to be achieved and all this is by His own design. Our humanity just knows that it is broken and needs the Lord, which leads us into a salvation walk that not only saves us but makes us intricate parts of God's plan. Our walk of salvation is not just purposed in our deliverance from past sins, but it is purposed in seeing us overcome and conquer future occurrences to give us the understanding of our union with Jesus Christ. We have now discussed many of the keys of salvation; faith, righteousness, justification, and grace. None of these is in operation alone or used for a single purpose, but they are intertwined in the salvation walk to produce God a people who are in relationship with Him yielding to His plans. Every time we obey and overcome our enemy we increase in the knowledge of Jesus Christ and move forward in our walk of salvation. We continue to be graced with more Truth and Spirit as we grow to the measure and stature of Jesus Christ (Ephesians 4:13, 1 John

3:2). This process of cutting off sin and becoming more like Jesus is found in the key of sanctification.

Sanctification is a specific key in the salvation walk which results in the intended purpose of people bearing the nature of Jesus Christ. Many people think that consecration and sanctification are the same thing, but they are quite different in how they work. The Hebrew word "qadash" (translated consecrate and sometimes sanctify) is an Old Testament word which means to be set apart to God's service, or to be set apart for God's use. While the Old Testament individuals used by God were set apart for his service, the lack of inward intimacy with the Spirit of God left them prone and vulnerable to the sin nature. This was remedied specifically by the Day of Atonement, and various offerings and cleansing rituals that would all be done away with through the atoning work of Christ Himself. The New Testament salvation walk is very different, in that it fully gives man the ability to overcome the sin through the inward work of the Holy Spirit. This sets God's people free from sin's mastery breaking man's slavery and bondage to sin (Romans 6:6,18-20, John 8:34). The New Testament word "hagiazō," or sanctify, means; to be pure and clean, to purify by sin expiation, both internally and externally. This specific key is used to prepare one for a greater work for Jesus Christ. It takes full understanding of the prior keys of salvation, justification and grace. These keys unlock the door of sanctification which is a state of deliverance.

The key of sanctification is not one that is optional. It is a necessity for those who are truly owned by and are in relationship with God. It is impossible to live in a relationship with God and not be set free from the issues that lead to sin. Once you come into relationship with God, the Holy Spirit is going to lead and guide you into all Truth (John 16:13, 1 John 2:27, 1 John 4:6). This guidance is going to set you free from sins mastery (John 8:32, Romans 8:2). That is the purpose of hearing the truth about your faults is to help you overcome them. If you refuse to hear the truth you will never be set free and your sin nature will continue to rule causing you to run from God. Running from God and the Truth is what gets you into trouble. This is why the salvation walk starts with repenting of sin, confessing the Lordship of Jesus and believing in your heart that He is a God of love. He is a God that wants to atone for your sin, while He teaches you to overcome them one by one by believing the Truth and walking in the Spirit. It is impossible to walk with Jesus and not defeat sin. It is impossible to walk with Him and not grow into His image. It is also impossible to walk with Jesus and not grow in hearing the truth. Fear of the truth is abandoned for an increase of God's love every time you acknowledge your fault and look to Jesus to help you overcome it. This process also gives you great compassion for others, since you realize you yourself are faulty. It also leads you to point them to Jesus because you realize only His love is willing to go with them through every obstacle. This is the salvation walk and each day you work on a growing union that leads you to be one with Him.

Hebrews 2:9

For both he that sanctifieth and they who are sanctified are all of one: for which cause he is not ashamed to call them brethren, Saying, I will declare thy name unto my brethren, in the midst of the church will I sing praise unto thee. And again, I will put my trust in him. And again, Behold I and the children which God hath given

John 17:17-19

Sanctify them through thy truth: thy word is truth. As thou hast sent me into the world, even so have I also sent them into the world. And for their sakes I sanctify myself, that they also might be sanctified through the truth. Neither pray I for these alone, but for them also which shall believe on me through their word; That they all may be one; as thou, Father, art in me, and I in thee, that they also may be one in us: that the world may believe that thou hast sent me.

I Corinthians 1:30

That no flesh should glory in his presence. But of him are ye in Christ Jesus, who of God is made unto us wisdom, and righteousness, and sanctification, and redemption: That, according as it is written, He that glorieth, let him glory in the Lord.

The key to understanding sanctification is to understand that Jesus wants you to rule and reign with Him. This is why Jesus ruled over the sin nature in His body and defeated every demon which would lead you astray. In John 17:19, you notice that He sanctified Himself so that you and I could be sanctified by the Truth. Jesus Christ is the Truth that sets you free. If God is willing to defeat sin for you, then who are you not to let Him speak His Truth into your life? Especially when His desire is to set you free from the sin, failure, and fault that has come to cause you pain. God is not only speaking to us by a still small voice, but He sends people full of Jesus into our lives to tell us truth. People who love us and have not come to destroy us, but to see us succeed. This is the will of God for every human; that they succeed in overcoming every issue through relationship with Him. This sanctification is not just to happen in one area of your life, but in all areas. Jesus is so intimate, He wants to help you in it all. When you allow Him ownership He will not only help you succeed, but people will see Him in your life and the earth will literally be filled with His glory. Sanctification is at work in all areas of your existence. This is why the Word of God deals with every issue in life.

I Thessalonians 5:23
And the very God of peace sanctify you wholly; and I pray God your whole spirit and soul and body be preserved blameless unto the coming of our Lord Jesus Christ. Faithful is he that calleth you, who also will do it.

I Thessalonians 4:3-7

For this is the will of God, even your sanctification, that ye should abstain from fornication: That every one of you should know how to possess his vessel in sanctification and honour; Not in the lust of concupiscence, even as the Gentiles which know not God: That no man go beyond and defraud his brother in any matter: because that the Lord is the avenger of all such, as we also have forewarned you and testified. For God hath not called us unto uncleanness, but unto holiness. He therefore that despiseth, despiseth not man, but God, who hath also given unto us his Holy Spirit.

When we think of the word fornication, we automatically think of sexual sin. But the word for fornication, in context with sanctification, is a spiritual analogy. Spiritual fornication is the act of letting the various lusts within the world draw you away from your relationship with Jesus Christ so you follow after and worship other spirits. Everyone must hear the truth about their areas of weakness and learn to take hold of their own vessels with sanctification and honor. You must let the Holy Spirit teach you to be clean. When you fail, you have the blood of Jesus, but you also need to hear the truth in love so you will be made an overcomer. The only way sanctification takes place is by hearing the truth and walking in the Spirit. This two-fold method is revealed in the following texts.

2 Thessalonians 2:13-14

But we are bound to give thanks alway to God for you, brethren beloved of the Lord, because God hath from the beginning chosen you to salvation through sanctification of the Spirit and belief of the truth: Whereunto he called you by our gospel, to the obtaining of the glory of our Lord Jesus Christ

I Peter 1:22-23

Seeing ye have purified your souls in obeying the truth through the Spirit unto unfeigned love of the brethren, see that ye love one another with a pure heart fervently: Being born again, not of corruptible seed, but of incorruptible, by the word of God, which liveth and abideth for ever.

This is why it is wrong for preachers to preach "tickle me Elmo" messages. These are feel good messages that tell everyone they qualify for the blessing without requiring people to evaluate their relationship with God. Without preaching the full knowledge of the Word, people are hindered from hearing the Truth and are left bound in sin. The world calls this "love." It is not real love because it stops the process of sanctification and victory. It is also wrong to stop the work of the Holy Spirit. He comes to make the Word real and intimate, dealing deep on the inside of man where the relationship with Jesus exists. This is the sanctified life; a place where love for the truth grows and the Holy Spirit moves to cause supernatural growth. Satan wants to stop your growth, he wants you to be embarrassed, hide, or feel fear so you will not acknowledge the truth. He knows if you continue in your relationship with God, he will lose his influence over your life. Those who continue in the salvation walk with Jesus Christ are truly saints.

We have been taught by denomination and manmade opinion that a saint is a perfect person who never sins. The Roman Catholic Church even takes sainthood to the level of praying to the individual declared to be a saint. Praying to a person won't make you like Jesus. Spending time with Jesus makes you like Jesus. He is not a fallen man, He is God in a body. The truth is, all the people you think are saints, simply made their relationship with Jesus Christ their number one goal. They were not sinless, rather they ruled over sin by obeying the Word and the Spirit. This process of sanctification validates your ability to become a true saint of God. As long as you are in this life, you will be dealing with an area that is not Christ-like. The very act of longing for sanctification and staying in relationship with Jesus qualifies you for sainthood. The word for saint in the Greek is "hagios." It means, "one with warm tender care for God that loves being clean." It also means, "sanctified one." To further summarize, it is someone who cuts off sin. It is this desire that proves you are one of the saints and a member of the household of God. If you are in relationship with Jesus Christ and you love to cut off sin's ownership in your life, you are a saint.

I Corinthians 1:2
Unto the church of God which is at Corinth, to them that are sanctified in Christ Jesus, called to be saints, with all that in

every place call upon the name of Jesus Christ our Lord, both theirs and ours.

2 Thessalonians 1:10
When he shall come to be glorified in his saints, and to be admired in all them that believe (because our testimony among you was believed) in that day.

Ephesians 1:18-19
The eyes of your understanding being enlightened; that ye may know what is the hope of his calling, and what the riches of the glory of his inheritance in the saints, and what [is] the exceeding greatness of his power to us-ward who believe, according to the working of his mighty power.

Ephesians 5:1-7
Be ye therefore followers of God, as dear children; and walk in love, as Christ also hath loved us, and hath given himself for us an offering and a sacrifice to God for a sweet smelling savour.But fornication, and all uncleanness, or covetousness, let it not be once named among you, as becometh saints; Neither filthiness, nor foolish talking, nor jesting, which are not convenient: but rather giving of thanks. For this ye know, that no whoremonger, nor unclean person, nor covetous man, who is an idolater, hath any inheritance in the kingdom of Christ and of God. Let no man deceive you with vain words: for because of these things cometh the wrath of God upon the children of disobedience. Be not ye therefore partakers with them.

As we keep our relationship with Jesus strong and our salvation walk on course, we move towards the fulfillment of God's divine plan. His plan is a beautiful union of Christ and the Church. It is this relationship that causes us to grow and meet Him in understanding, knowledge, and stature. We allow His Truth to judge us and we are become transformed to be like Him. This is why judgment starts in the house of the Lord. The assembly of the saints is the place we allow God to teach us His Word so the Holy Spirit can judge our hearts. It is not the arm of the flesh that judges us. It is the Word of God which is the truth that was spoken by Jesus (John 12:48, Hebrews 12:25, john 14:15, 21). It is who He is and we should desire to be like Him. People who don't want to hear the Truth of God's Word will always quote "judge not lest ye be judged." What they fail to realize is that those who are in relationship with God allow His Word and Spirit to judge them constantly.

I Corinthians 6:1-8

Dare any of you, having a matter against another, go to law before the unjust, and not before the saints? Do ye not know that the saints shall judge the world? and if the world shall be judged by you, are ye unworthy to judge the smallest matters? Know ye not that we shall judge angels? how much more things that pertain to this life? If then ye have judgments of things pertaining to this life, set them to judge who are least esteemed in the church. I speak to your shame. Is it so, that there is not a wise man among you? no, not one that shall be able to judge between his brethren? But brother goeth to law with brother, and that before the unbelievers. Now therefore there is utterly a fault among you, because ye go to law one with another. Why do ye not rather take wrong? why do ye not rather suffer yourselves to be defrauded? Nay, ye do wrong, and defraud, and that your brethren.

Saints are willing to receive the truth about themselves so they can be set free. If you ask someone to live what you are not living yourself, then what you preach is coming back to you. This is why you need to understand that you cannot help people in areas you are not overcoming through obedience to Jesus yourself. True saints love to hear the truth of God's Word, allowing it to search them internally until they respond with a deeper love for Jesus and others. The process of sanctification is preparing God's saints and it is destined for a purpose. The purpose is the day of the saints. Any real relationship requires that the truth be spoken for it to grow. Sometimes the process is painful for those speaking the truth as well as for those hearing it. It hurts to know the faults and weakness of those you love, it also hurts to admit you have fault and weakness. This is why love is the answer to walk with people. Only love will keep you in a relationship with people when it is painful. This love is learned from Jesus, who experienced the maximum amount of pain and still conquered it all by love. We are being prepared to reign with Jesus because as saints we know the issues of this life and its sin, but we also know that every man is given the opportunity to overcome it by a relationship with Jesus Christ. The true purpose of the salvation walk is to develop, for God, a people who will fulfill His will. The final culmination of this will is mentioned to us in the following texts:

Jude 1:14-15

And Enoch also, the seventh from Adam, prophesied of these, saying, Behold, the Lord cometh with ten thousands of his saints, To execute judgment upon all, and to convince all that are ungodly among them of all their ungodly deeds which they have ungodly committed, and of all their hard speeches which ungodly sinners have spoken against him.

Daniel 7:17-28

These great beasts, which are four, are four kings, which shall arise out of the earth. But the saints of the most High shall take the kingdom, and possess the kingdom for ever, even for ever and ever. Then I would know the truth of the fourth beast, which was diverse from all the others, exceeding dreadful, whose teeth were of iron, and his nails of brass; which devoured, brake in pieces, and stamped the residue with his feet; And of the ten horns that were in his head, and of the other which came up, and before whom three fell; even of that horn that had eyes, and a mouth that spake very great things, whose look was more stout than his fellows. I beheld, and the same horn made war with the saints, and prevailed against them; Until the Ancient of days came, and judgment was given to the saints of the most High; and the time came that the saints possessed the kingdom. Thus he said, The fourth beast shall be the fourth kingdom upon earth, which shall be diverse from all kingdoms, and shall devour the whole earth, and shall tread it down, and break it in pieces. And the ten horns out of this kingdom are ten kings that shall arise: and another shall rise after them; and he shall be diverse from the first, and he shall subdue three kings. And he shall speak great words against the most High, and shall wear out the saints of the most High, and think to change times and laws: and they shall be given into his hand until a time and times and the dividing of time. But the judgment shall sit, and they shall take away his dominion, to consume and to destroy it unto the end. And the kingdom and dominion, and the greatness of the kingdom under the whole heaven, shall be given to the people of the saints of the most High, whose kingdom is an everlasting kingdom, and all dominions shall serve and obey him. Hitherto is the end of the matter. As for me Daniel, my cogitations much troubled me, and my countenance changed in me: but I kept the matter in my heart.

The real salvation walk does not start when you get to heaven; it is active and at work in those with relationship with Jesus right now. Not only is sanctification preparing a people, but it is teaching those people how to overcome and walk in victory. You are moving from faith to faith and glory to glory; overcoming enemies through the working of Jesus Christ from the heart. As you go through salvation, justification, grace, and sanctification, understand that you are going through preparation. You are being prepared for Jesus himself. God not only teaches the saints through the Word and the Spirit, He also calls them to experience real life application by ministering to others and being ministered to themselves. You cannot really understand who Jesus is without developing relationship with God and man. Sanctification is happening and it is calling the saints to deal with issues that come up in their salvation walk while having relationship with God and man. I want to leave you with a text from Ephesians 4 that gives you the goal of our transformation:

Ephesians 4:10-32
He that descended is the same also that ascended up far above all heavens, that he might fill all things.) And he gave some, apostles; and some, prophets; and some, evangelists; and some, pastors and teachers; For the perfecting of the saints, for the work of the ministry, for the edifying of the body of Christ: Till we all come in the unity of the faith, and of the knowledge of the Son of God, unto a perfect man, unto the measure of the stature of the fulness of Christ:
That we henceforth be no more children, tossed to and fro, and carried about with every wind of doctrine, by the sleight of men, and cunning craftiness, whereby they lie in wait to deceive; But speaking the truth in love, may grow up into him in all things, which is the head, even Christ: From whom the whole body fitly joined together and compacted by that which every joint supplieth, according to the effectual working in the measure of every part, maketh increase of the body unto the edifying of itself in love. This I say therefore, and testify in the Lord, that ye henceforth walk not as other Gentiles walk, in the

vanity of their mind, Having the understanding darkened, being alienated from the life of God through the ignorance that is in them, because of the blindness of their heart: Who being past feeling have given themselves over unto lasciviousness, to work all uncleanness with greediness. But ye have not so learned Christ; If so be that ye have heard him, and have been taught by him, as the truth is in Jesus: That ye put off concerning the former conversation the old man, which is corrupt according to the deceitful lusts; And be renewed in the spirit of your mind; And that ye put on the new man, which after God is created in righteousness and true holiness. Wherefore putting away lying, speak every man truth with his neighbour: for we are members one of another. Be ye angry, and sin not: let not the sun go down upon your wrath: Neither give place to the devil. Let him that stole steal no more: but rather let him labour, working with [his] hands the thing which is good, that he may have to give to him that needeth. Let no corrupt communication proceed out of your mouth, but that which is good to the use of edifying, that it may minister grace unto the hearers. And grieve not the Holy Spirit of God, whereby ye are sealed unto the day of redemption. Let all bitterness, and wrath, and anger, and clamour, and evil speaking, be put away from you, with all malice: And be ye kind one to another, tenderhearted, forgiving one another, even as God for Christ's sake hath forgiven you.

Chapter 8

Taking the Saints to Holiness

Sanctification leads us to the next key of our salvation walk which is holiness. The actual word for saint in the Greek is "hagios" it is translated as "saint," sixty-one times as "holy," one-hundred-sixty-one times and "Holy One" three times. I point this out because this word is the "Holy" in front of "Holy Spirit" and "Holy Ghost," and even references to Jesus as "Holy One." It is the core relational principle for us in the salvation walk moving into sainthood. We cannot spend time with a Holy God and not have holy rub off on us. The same word is used for holy ground, holy angels, holy Jerusalem, holy city. These locations take on the characteristic of "holy" because this is where man meets with God or hear His message. The truth is, saints are holy people. They love the feeling of being clean on the inside. They love to have clean hands and a pure heart.

Many denominations and individuals have tried to achieve holiness by outward dress and outward works. This type of thinking misses the fundamental purpose of holiness. God is not seeking a relationship with a Kleenex, prayer cloth or any earthly article. He is seeking a relationship with the person who longs to be as He is. The only way a Kleenex becomes holy is when it is used to dry the tears of a saint seeking God from within. You must be aware, the Kleenex with the tears on it just reminds the saint to spend more time with God. It cannot change the heart of the saint. That happens within. The saints enjoys holiness because they love the feeling of being in God's presence. True holiness is this longing to keep a clean relationship with God; a heart condition from within the person who is in intimate relationship with God. You must be very careful not think that holiness is in any earthly article or work lest you get off course and start worshipping the work itself instead of God. Outward holiness and works are very dangerous because this substitute can make the person feel better than others, because the outward works result can be pride. Pride is the opposite of true holiness. True holiness from within understands that the only way to become holy is to be like the Jesus Himself. The saint longs to be so full of the Spirit of God that wrong internal feelings or thoughts are driven out. This is why the salvation walk is an increasing heart relationship with the Spirit. As the relationship grows internal feelings and thoughts are judged by God Himself from within.

Galatians 3:1-3
O foolish Galatians, who hath bewitched you, that ye should not obey the truth, before whose eyes Jesus Christ hath been evidently set forth, crucified among you? This only would I learn of you, Received ye the Spirit by the works of the law, or by the hearing of faith? Are ye so foolish? having begun in the Spirit, are ye now made perfect by the flesh?

1 Thessalonians 3:12-13

And the Lord make you to increase and abound in love one toward another, and toward all men, even as we do toward you: To the end he may stablish your hearts unblameable in holiness before God, even our Father, at the coming of our Lord Jesus Christ with all his saints.

While the outward articles are not where the problem exists, the old sin nature can cause people to go after the things of the world. Every individual must be aware of their personal responses concerning things that would lead them away. Many people fail to understand that, when God asks us to give up something outwardly or set certain boundaries concerning worldly influence, He is usually dealing with us reigning over the sin nature from within. Sanctified people also set boundaries concerning the outside influences of the world, because they have an extreme distaste for demonic influence. The saint wants to be clean, pure and holy because the dirt just leads people to sin and drift away from God. Every person in a walk with Christ will have internal conviction and individual reasons for what God asks of them outwardly. Holiness starts from the inside out; without the inside relationship, all that is done outwardly to prove one is holy is purely in vain.

Sanctification is when the Holy Spirit teaches you to conquer the practice of sin in your life. It starts with one sin, and as you continue to grow your relationship with God, you will cut off more sin. This is why the Bible says the way is narrow

(Matthew 7:13-14, John 14:6). As you grow with Christ, the wide way of living goes away and He deals with you about every aspect of your life. I told you that the word saint means "sanctified one." This is simply an individual who has developed the pattern of sanctification by cutting off sin. As the saint is taught this process, every victory moves you into the purification process called Holiness. Jesus Christ has all power and desires, through the work of the Holy Spirit, to lead every believer into the state of holiness. Your salvation walk is leading you to defeat your enemies and learn the ways of God. One of the best representations of the work of Jesus Christ is verbalized to us in a prophecy given to John by his father, Zachariah. Let's look at this prophecy in Luke chapter 1.

Luke 1:74
That he would grant unto us, that we being delivered out of the hand of our enemies might serve him without fear, In holiness and righteousness before him, all the days of our life. And thou, child, shalt be called the prophet of the Highest: for thou shalt go before the face of the Lord to prepare his ways; To give knowledge of salvation unto his people by the remission of their sins, Through the tender mercy of our God; whereby the dayspring from on high hath visited us, To give light to them that sit in darkness and in the shadow of death, to guide our feet into the way of peace.

The true purpose of our salvation walk is to learn to serve God without fear. Our relationship with Jesus allows us to be reunited to the Spirit resulting in God's righteousness and holiness being established in our lives. This is through the powerful work of remission of sins which brings us to the light, dispels the darkness, and guides us in the way of peace. After being in the presence of Jesus, the prostitute (about to be stoned) and the lame man at the pool of Bethesda are both given instructions after they experienced God's true nature of healing and preservation (John 5:14, John 8:11). Jesus says, "Go and sin no more." He also adds in one of the accounts, "Lest something worse come upon you." Some people view this as a threat. But it is not a threat; it is a reality that happens when we continue in our sin. God does not want anything worse to come upon you. He wants your life to be good and whole, happy and free. In both accounts, Jesus had already set each of these individuals free and blessed them with His Spirit. It is being in His presence that sets us free and this alone makes us long for His holiness. After being with Jesus we will repeat the words from Psalms 19:7-12, "The law of the LORD is perfect, converting the soul: the testimony of the LORD is sure, making wise the simple. The statutes of the LORD are right, rejoicing the heart: the commandment of the LORD is pure, enlightening the eyes. The fear of the LORD is clean, enduring for ever: the judgments of the LORD are true and righteous altogether. More to be desired are they than gold, yea, than much fine gold: sweeter also than honey and the honeycomb. Moreover by them is thy servant warned: [and] in keeping of them there is great reward. Who can understand his errors? cleanse thou me from secret faults." This text demonstrates the feelings of a saint concerning God's way. The relationship of

God at work in our lives is powerful and Jesus desires to purify us and make us clean. All we have to do is yield to Him and walk in relationship with Him and His purity will come forth in our life. Instead of using our bodies to sin, we will learn to follow Jesus and let Him own us for His purposes.

Romans 6:16-23

Know ye not, that to whom ye yield yourselves servants to obey, his servants ye are to whom ye obey; whether of sin unto death, or of obedience unto righteousness? But God be thanked, that ye were the servants of sin, but ye have obeyed from the heart that form of doctrine which was delivered you. Being then made free from sin, ye became the servants of righteousness. I speak after the manner of men because of the infirmity of your flesh: for as ye have yielded your members servants to uncleanness and to iniquity unto iniquity; even so now yield your members servants to righteousness unto holiness. For when ye were the servants of sin, ye were free from righteousness. What fruit had ye then in those things whereof ye are now ashamed? for the end of those things is death. But now being made free from sin, and become servants to God, ye have your fruit unto holiness, and the end everlasting life. For the wages of sin is death; but the gift of God is eternal life through Jesus Christ our Lord.

Those of us who long for holiness recognize the need for correction. The ultimate correction we can receive in your life is from God Himself. Relationship with God is to have access to our creator who has a perfect desire to see us overcome. The

Word of God and the work of the Spirit are works of love that also correct us when we yield to God's presence. God has no intention to destroy us with His correction; He comes to heal, protect and restore. Holiness is the state where the believer longs to be corrected to live. It is the state where we find life to the fullest and the benefits that follow. With no correction from the Lord, we limit His ability to cause us to walk upright and grow into His nature and image. Sometimes the walk of salvation will cause us to feel pain. But in the end, the benefits outweigh the small price we have to pay by hearing the Truth. God paid the penalty for our failures in full; it should be a pleasure to endure a little disciplinary pain or discomfort as He speaks His Words of Truth. His discipline comes for our good and not our harm. When we yield to God, it takes us to new levels in Christ and greater heights in our walk into holiness.

Hebrews 12:6-17

For whom the Lord loveth he chasteneth, and scourgeth every son whom he receiveth. If ye endure chastening, God dealeth with you as with sons; for what son is he whom the father chasteneth not? But if ye be without chastisement, whereof all are partakers, then are ye bastards, and not sons. Furthermore we have had fathers of our flesh which corrected us, and we gave them reverence: shall we not much rather be in subjection unto the Father of spirits, and live? For they verily for a few days chastened us after their own pleasure; but he for our profit, that we might be partakers of his holiness. Now no chastening for the present seemeth to be joyous, but grievous: nevertheless afterward it yieldeth the peaceable fruit of righteousness unto them which are exercised thereby. Wherefore lift up the hands which hang down, and the feeble knees; And make straight paths for your feet, lest that which is lame be turned out of the way; but let it rather be healed. Follow peace with all men, and holiness, without which no man shall see the Lord: Looking diligently lest any man fail of the grace of God; lest any root of bitterness springing up trouble you, and thereby many be defiled; Lest there be any fornicator, or profane person, as Esau, who for one morsel of meat sold his birthright. For ye know how that afterward, when he would have inherited the blessing, he was rejected: for he found no place of repentance, though he sought it carefully with tears.

1 Peter 1:13-16
Wherefore gird up the loins of your mind, be sober, and hope to the end for the grace that is to be brought unto you at the revelation of Jesus Christ; As obedient children, not fashioning yourselves according to the former lusts in your ignorance: But as he which hath called you is holy, so be ye holy in all manner of conversation; Because it is written, Be ye holy; for I am holy.

The key to holiness is to never give up on your relationship with Jesus. It is in this relationship you show your true heart toward God. God will always be the mark of perfection you strive to attain and, as we seek His ways, He is the one who does the perfecting. Many people think that perfect means a state of complete sinlessness, but this state is found in God alone. He alone is perfect. You are being brought into union with Him so that you can learn His ways and be complete. John 17:23 says, "I in them, and thou in me, that they may be made perfect in one; and that the world may know that thou hast sent me, and hast loved them, as thou hast loved me." In the Salvation Walk chapter, it was established that "they that endure to the end shall be saved." The word "end" is "telos," which means "to sell out for a definite finishing point or goal." This word is the root word for, "perfect." The word "perfect" in Greek is "teleios." It means "to mature and be brought to a state of completion by finishing to the end." To God, the state of completion is for you to stay in relationship with Him, desiring His ways until the end of your natural life. There is no death in Christ, only the final state of complete perfection that we have longed for since we came in contact with our God. It is that place of wanting to put on the complete perfection of God that is the ultimate work of holiness. You must desire to put it on and seek it as you grow in relationship with Christ. In this God is pleased and your heart is secure in keeping the greatest relationship man has ever known. God has made the way and has set the path. This path will keep you from the devourer and bring about the completion of your eternal redemption. It is called the highway of holiness.

Isaiah 35:8-9
And an highway shall be there, and a way, and it shall be called The way of holiness; the unclean shall not pass over it; but it shall be for those: the wayfaring men, though fools, shall not err

[therein]. No lion shall be there, nor any ravenous beast shall go up thereon, it shall not be found there; but the redeemed shall walk there

Holiness the final key to understanding the salvation walk. It is in this final key that we find the goal and completion of our salvation, so that we stand before the Lord knowing we have held our relationship with Him in its proper position; loving every victory He obtained for us and understanding that His desire is for us to be like Him. Our walk is daily, our heart is set. We are determined to live this life in the presence of the Lord as well as the eternal one to come.

2 Corinthians 7:1
Having therefore these promises, dearly beloved, let us cleanse ourselves from all filthiness of the flesh and spirit, perfecting holiness in the fear of God.

This is the salvation walk, and the ultimate desire is to become like Jesus through the Total walk of salvation. It has a beginning and an ending, but the key is your desire to be as He is. May the Lord increase all of us to know Him more, experience His victory, and learn His principles, so we can bear the heart of love to Him and all of humanity who desperately need this relationship of fulfillment. God needs you to be filled with His Spirit of love to be like Him, and you need God to teach you to overcome. This is a picture of true relationship, and we win on both sides.